The Cartoonist's Workbook

Robin Hall

Main Street
A division of Sterling Publishing Co., Inc.
New York

Library of Congress Cataloging-in-Publication Data Available

4 6 8 10 9 7 5

Published 2004 by Sterling Publishing Co., Inc.
387 Park Avenue South, New York, NY 10016
Originally published 1995 in Great Britain
© 1995 by Robin Hall
Distributed in Canada by Sterling Publishing
c/o Canadian Manda Group, 165 Dufferin Street
Toronto, Ontario, Canada M6K 3H6

Sterling ISBN 13: 978-1-4027-1608-9
ISBN 10: 1-4027-1608-7

For information about custom editions, special sales, premium and
corporate purchases, please contact Sterling Special Sales
Department at 800-805-5489 or specialsales@sterlingpub.com

Contents

Acknowledgments

Many thanks to:

my brother and partner in crime Peter Hall, whose brilliant cartoons have always inspired me:

my brother Michael Hall for making the book comprehensible and committing it to disk;

Pat McGhee, Gary Hamilton and Ronnie Baird for their help and encouragement;

Maggie Dun, Jon Kimble, Jim Russell and everyone at Knight Features for helping me on my way;

Anne Watts, my favorite editor;

and Niki McPherson – I'd be lost without you.

Preface

Cartooning always appealed to me because I assumed that most cartoonists didn't have to get up early in the morning. Well, that's not the full story: I was also fascinated by the way that cartoons were able to encapsulate all aspects of human life – from the serious to the humorous, the earth-shattering to the mundane – in one frozen image.

However, I wasn't one of those lucky people born with bundles of creative ability. In fact, I couldn't draw a cartoon to save my life; even my stick figures looked unshapely. If I was to get into cartooning I knew that I'd have to do some serious work. So I studied every cartoon I could lay my hands on, hundreds of them, and I practiced and practiced . . . and practiced.

As my work improved, I began to realize that, if I followed certain guidelines and shortcuts when creating a cartoon, satisfactory results were almost guaranteed. Gradually, I developed these guidelines and shortcuts into a method which finally opened the door for me into the cartooning world.

This book is my attempt to share this method with all those who, like myself, are full of enthusiasm but short on natural ability. For beginners and professionals alike, I have added a wealth of reference material which I hope will be of lasting value. I wish all you budding cartoonists good luck, and if you make it, it's true, you WON'T have to get up so early in the morning!

Robin Hall

Drawing Cartoons as Easy as ABC

Drawing cartoons – as easy as A B C

The process of drawing cartoons can be likened to that of writing (or "drawing") the alphabet. You don't need a special talent, just some useful guidelines and a LOT of practice.

For instance, when you learned the alphabet, you were probably told that to make an "A" you had to join two lines together in a point, "like a church steeple," and then connect these lines with another one drawn horizontally.

In other words, you had to "draw" /\   then   A

And then came the important bit – you were made to REPEAT this hundreds of times until you could do it with ease.

Now, with cartooning, it is the same type of "process," only with new guidelines. For instance, to draw a face, I could tell you to begin by drawing a "C", flattened a bit, like a sausage:

Next, add 2 dots just above the right-hand corner:

Then draw a line down from the middle of the flattened "C":

Now draw a "reverse C" opposite the flattened one:

Then draw some angled lines above the right-hand dot:

Finally, draw a line for a mouth – and you've drawn a face!

Now comes the important part – PRACTICE this!

Keyhole Ken – the cartoon character

Now let's use the same process to draw a basic human cartoon figure which we can later expand upon.

Begin with a keyhole shape by drawing a circle with a "box" shape under it (the sides of which "move in" towards the top).

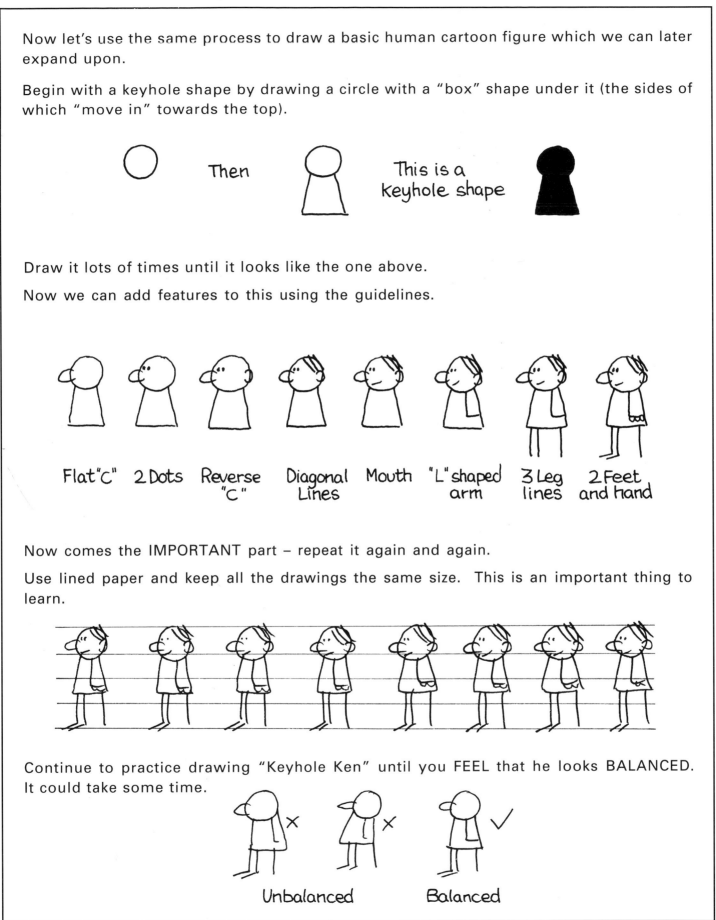

Draw it lots of times until it looks like the one above.

Now we can add features to this using the guidelines.

Flat "C"   2 Dots   Reverse "C"   Diagonal Lines   Mouth   "L" shaped arm   3 Leg lines   2 Feet and hand

Now comes the IMPORTANT part – repeat it again and again.

Use lined paper and keep all the drawings the same size. This is an important thing to learn.

Continue to practice drawing "Keyhole Ken" until you FEEL that he looks BALANCED. It could take some time.

Unbalanced   Balanced

After you have practiced drawing Keyhole Ken facing in one direction, draw him facing the other way.

REMEMBER – PRACTICE, PRACTICE, PRACTICE.

So instead of this ← draw him this way →

Now, to make things more interesting we can begin to draw people of different heights. For instance, say you wanted to draw a tall friend beside Ken, first draw Ken then begin his friend higher up.

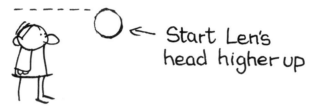

← Start Len's head higher up

Now remember, if a person is tall EVERYTHING must be taller so obviously the following can't work:

} This needs to be extended down to the ground

} extended

Now PRACTICE this over and over again on lined paper.

How to draw Keyhole Ken from all angles

Cartoon characters must be able to face and look in ALL directions. There are 3 basic body poses that will allow the head to look ANYWHERE.

You already know 2 of the body poses – facing left and facing right. The 3rd one is facing TOWARDS us.

First draw the keyhole shape:

Now, as before, you need to add a nose, eyes, ears, hair, mouth, arms, legs and feet. First of all just LOOK at the "keyhole" and IMAGINE where these features would be if Ken were facing towards you. Then go through the usual process but draw each feature where you IMAGINE it should be.

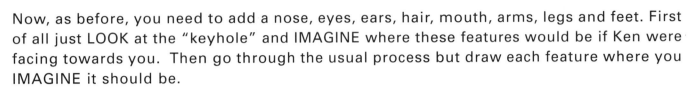

nose   eyes   ears   hair   mouth   arms   legs   feet

REMEMBER – these are the same features turned around to face TOWARDS us.

Before beginning the face, you can make Ken look in ANY direction you want by "pointing" his nose in that direction.

Now go through the process of building up the face by using the nose to help you PICTURE where the eyes, ears, hair and mouth are to be drawn.

Some poses

ARMS

relaxed   "Oh yea!"   "Sorry"   "WHAT!"   "Don't know"

"Oh, oh!"   "Mmm..."   "AAARGH!"   "Now let me see"   "Over there"

LEGS

relaxed   walking   running   skidding

sitting   kicking   sitting   leaning

FULL BODY

fallen down   running   "on all fours"

REMEMBER – PRACTICE, PRACTICE, PRACTICE.

Keyhole costumes

Let's see how we can draw ANY COSTUME using the keyhole shape as a guide.

Ken already has a "coat" shape, so to begin with you could change this to various coats and tops using the keyhole shape to help you IMAGINE the item you desire.

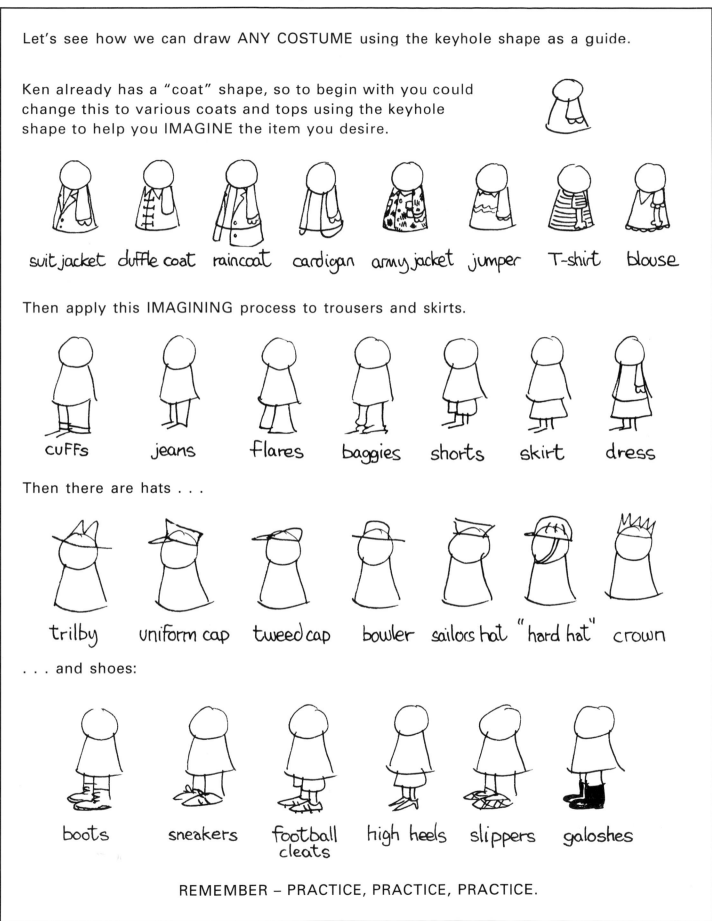

suit jacket   duffle coat   raincoat   cardigan   army jacket   jumper   T-shirt   blouse

Then apply this IMAGINING process to trousers and skirts.

cuffs   jeans   flares   baggies   shorts   skirt   dress

Then there are hats . . .

trilby   uniform cap   tweed cap   bowler   sailors hat   "hard hat"   crown

. . . and shoes:

boots   sneakers   football cleats   high heels   slippers   galoshes

REMEMBER – PRACTICE, PRACTICE, PRACTICE.

Some additional features

Remember, practice these facing the other way as well.

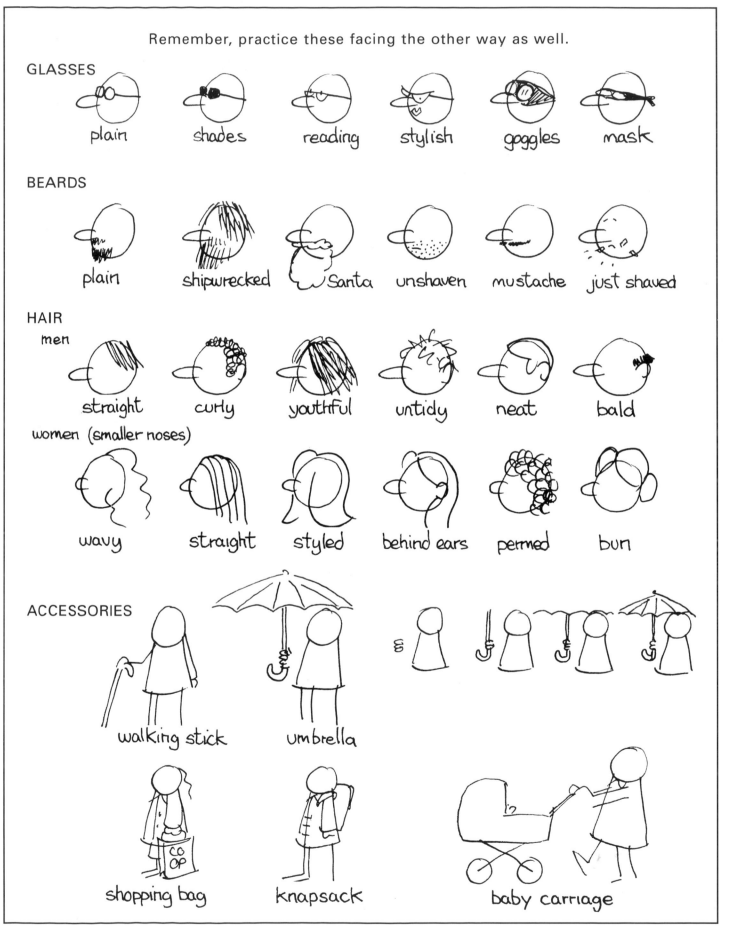

GLASSES

plain   shades   reading   stylish   goggles   mask

BEARDS

plain   shipwrecked   Santa   unshaven   mustache   just shaved

HAIR

men

straight   curly   youthful   untidy   neat   bald

women (smaller noses)

wavy   straight   styled   behind ears   permed   bun

ACCESSORIES

walking stick   umbrella

shopping bag   knapsack   baby carriage

A collection of keyhole characters to practice

First, draw lots of keyhole shapes, then while LOOKING at the keyhole IMAGINE ("picture") the costume you want and draw in the more obvious features.

Through the ages

Here are a few ways to make your characters look their age.

BABIES
large head
rounded body
can't stand up

small nose
big eyes
big ears
not much hair

CHILDREN
scruffy hair
small body
small nose
big ears
T-shirt, shorts
sneakers

young hairstyle
very neat
small nose
cute clothes
sensible shoes

TEENAGERS
quite tall
fashionable
rebellious

THIRTY-SOMETHING
tidier
more conservative
practical
"sensible" clothes
stylish

MIDDLE-AGED
comfortable clothing
heavier build
shorter
weary look
slightly ruffled
more hunched over

ELDERLY
any old clothes
shorter again
thinner
very hunched over
face "squashed"
false teeth?
childlike expression

Expressions

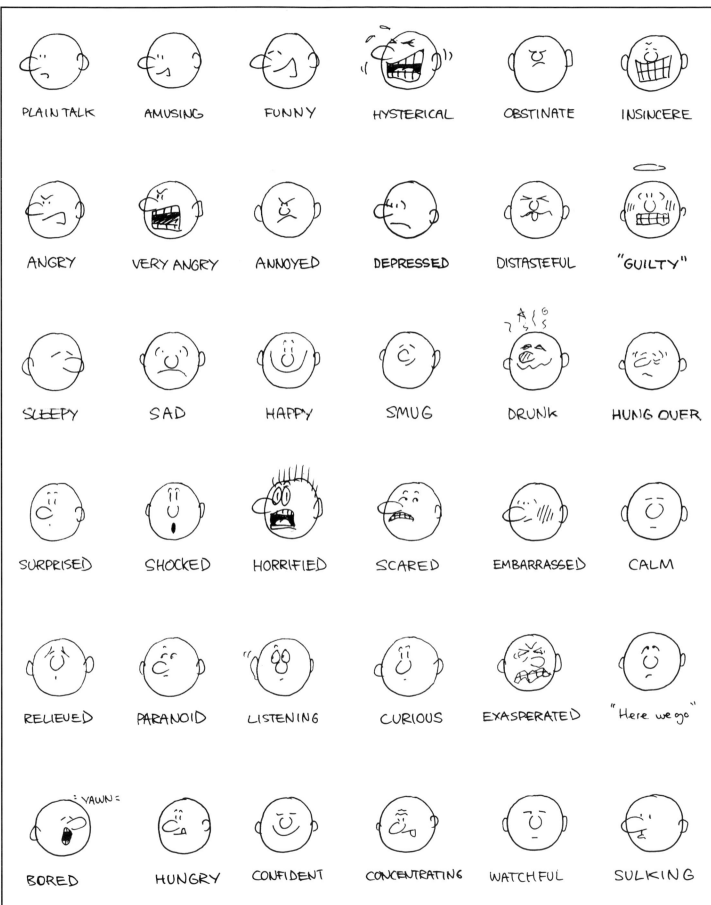

It's true what they say – practice makes perfect – but don't make it a CHORE or you'll get fed up.

Try to keep the equipment you need to practice your cartoons as near at hand as possible. Sometimes the THOUGHT of having to get things ready is enough to make you turn on the television.

EQUIPMENT – Obtain a cheap HARDBACK exercise book (LINED) that you can easily sit on your knee. DON'T buy an expensive sketchbook – you'll be afraid to scribble! And keep some pens handy.

Now don't sit too long wondering what to draw – just START the flow by drawing something basic like Keyhole Ken. Repeat it over and over again. Be QUICK.

Then maybe try it facing in the other direction.

Then you could try EXPRESSION only. Draw lots of circles, then QUICKLY add expressions.

Next you could try COSTUMES. Draw lots of Keyhole Ken shapes, then QUICKLY try some costumes.

Finally try different basic poses – running, walking, etc., etc. . . . .

Now that you can draw Ken in many poses and with various expressions you can begin to change him into any character you wish.

Let's begin with the face.

Each feature on Ken's face can be altered to depict a certain type of person.

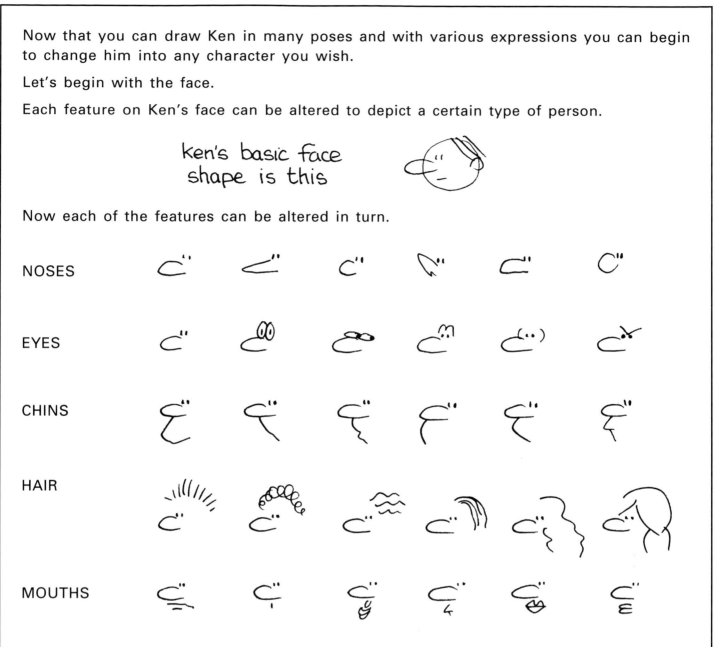

ken's basic face shape is this

Now each of the features can be altered in turn.

NOSES

EYES

CHINS

HAIR

MOUTHS

Now to build a character, IMAGINE each feature. Say, for instance, you wanted to draw a sly villain with a pointed nose, "slit" eyes, no chin, slicked-back hair and shady looking (tense).

Make your way through the process of building a face using the type of features you've imagined.

pointy nose   "slit" eyes   no chin   slicked hair   "tense" shoulders

Study other cartoon characters to see how features are built up and practice copying them.

Developing complete keyhole characters

Let's say you want to draw two cowboys – a "good guy" and a "bad guy" who are competing for the attentions of a rancher's daughter, Emmy-Lou.

First IMAGINE how they MIGHT look in a typical western.

Good guy – tall, strong chin, well built, confident, dressed in white
Bad guy – short, no chin, stooped over, sneaky eyes, dressed in black
Emmy-Lou – medium height, hair in a ponytail, flowery dress

Now, start by drawing the good guy's BASIC keyhole shape (with legs).

Now we can call this height TALL

The bad guy is short so his head is lower.

The girl is medium so her head is in between and she'll be thinner

Drawn close together we have:

ROUGHLY add cowboy gear and a dress for Emmy-Lou.

Now add basic expressions.

exaggerate certain features

arm on hip - confident

chest out

back tensed up

dress

When you practice all this, be quick and loose. Don't worry if it looks scribbly, you can easily tidy it up by tracing it.

How to turn keyhole characters into finished cartoons

You now have 3 keyhole characters which look very sketchy.

One way to draw a "finished" cartoon from the keyhole sketch is to trace over it and only draw in IMPORTANT lines.

For example, the good guy's head would be traced by going through the process for building a face so that only IMPORTANT lines are drawn. Use tracing paper, or thin white paper if you can see through it.

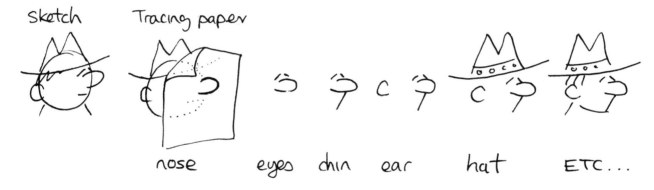

Sketch   Tracing paper

nose   eyes   chin   ear   hat   ETC...

Also WHEN TRACING you can exaggerate certain features.

So

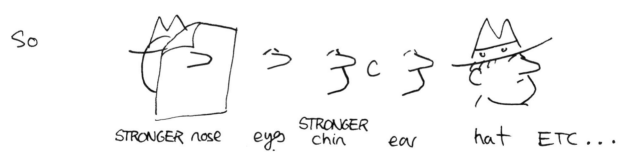

STRONGER nose   eyes   STRONGER chin   ear   hat   ETC...

If you continue this process with the 3 characters, you could end up (after a lot of practice) with this:

Special effects

There are plenty of books that cover this subject in detail so rather than repeat it all, I'll just go over a few simple "tricks" that can be used to good effect.

GROUND SHADOWS

A simple shadow can give a character a greater sense of being GROUNDED, rather than floating in "whiteness."

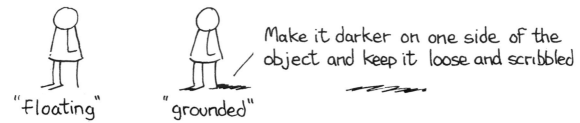

Make it darker on one side of the object and keep it loose and scribbled

These shadows can also indicate WHERE a character is in relation to the ground.

They can also give objects in midair more solidity and "height."

OBJECT SHADOWS

The simple rule to follow is to shade an object on the side farthest away from the light source (YOU pick the light source – it's your cartoon).
For example

Special effects – movement lines

When objects move, we see a "sweeping" image, not just "one" image. Check this out by waving your hand around.

In a cartoon, we show this "sweeping" movement by drawing lines in the DIRECTION of the movement ("sweep lines").

SWEEP LINES

But also, to make it clear what these lines indicate we need to add a few more lines to represent the OBJECT at various points along its line of travel.

OBJECT LINES

The curved lines represent the object at previous stages

If an object is waving about in ALL directions, we can add just a few "object" lines to indicate this.

The general rule is – if you want to indicate small movement then just draw in some OBJECT LINES in the places the object has moved through.

If you want to indicate a larger sweeping movement then draw in SWEEP LINES to indicate direction AND some OBJECT LINES (usually close to the object) to indicate that the object is moving.

small movement
OBJECT LINES

SWEEP LINES AND OBJECT LINES
help to make this movement clearer

A keyhole crowd

A good thing to practice is crowd scenes to force you to think about different heights, expressions, poses, clothing, etc.

Although it's actually quite easy, the finished product is often impressive looking.

First – think HEADS and draw some (not all) of them at different heights. IMAGINE the heads within a crowd and QUICKLY draw them in relation to where you think the ground might be.

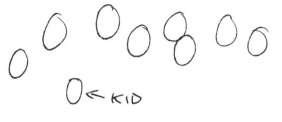

Now draw in keyhole bodies and JUST THE OUTER LINES of the legs. Don't add feet yet.

Now GIVE THEM ALL A DIRECTION TO FACE IN.

Use the NOSES to "point the way."

Now you can draw in the extra leg line as well (and feet).

Finally, simply keep building up costumes, expressions and whatever else comes to mind. Don't OVERDO it. People don't really dress THAT differently.

"Keyhole" animals

The rules that we have applied to cartoon people can also be applied to cartoon animals. Let's begin with the face process.

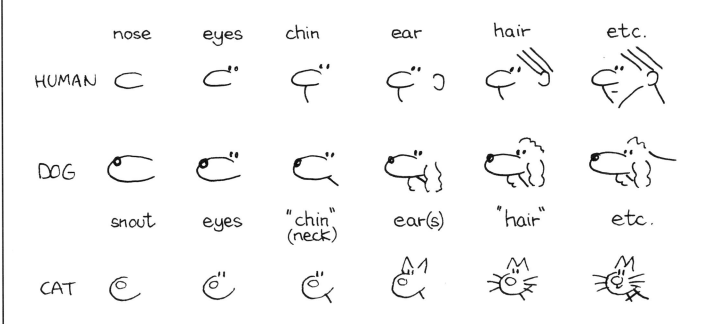

Now see if you can use this process to draw the following assortment of animal faces.

bird   cow   mouse   alligator

For animal bodies we can still use the keyhole technique but more often than not we will want to keep it in mind rather than draw it out. The thing to remember is that animals have similar shapes to human beings but everything is bent over as if we were touching the ground with our hands.

We could use this IMAGE to draw a "keyhole" cat.

Animal essentials

The one thing most beginners forget about with cartoon animals is to draw in their NECKS.

Most beginners draw this:

 but ALL animals have longish necks

After the neck is in place THEN we draw in the back and legs. Quick cartoon legs can simply be like very thin human legs (and add on a 'thigh' to the back legs).

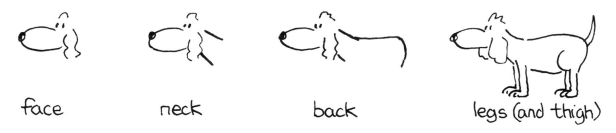

face   neck   back   legs (and thigh)

You can see this process in many animals. Try to draw them.

Use the keyhole technique if you want a QUICK idea of an image you have in mind. Change it to suit each animal. Use it as a reference sketch. Picture in your mind the most BASIC shape of the animal you wish to draw and sketch it out QUICKLY. Then USE this as a guide for a more detailed drawing.

cow   cat   dog

Raining cats and dogs

Here are some typical poses and some essential features for our most popular cartoon animals. Remember – always practice drawing things in the other direction as well.

feet

upright

long whiskers

short whiskers

long haired

thin

fat

Advanced Drawing Techniques

Drawing without picture reference

The ultimate goal in cartooning is to be able to draw any image that comes into your head without having to spend three hours looking through half a dozen encyclopedias for reference.

To do this you first have to learn to VISUALIZE an image in mind. You have to play detective. Analyze the object, see it in sections, shapes, sizes. Imagine you are actually looking at the object, as if you could touch it. Try to bring the image in your mind more into focus.

After you have done this you can use any or all of the following techniques to get your image down on paper.

1   BREAK THE IMAGE DOWN TO BASIC SHAPES

2   DRAW A "FRAMEWORK" TO USE AS GUIDELINES

Drawing without picture reference

3   BUILD OUTWARDS FROM ONE SECTION OF THE OBJECT
In the same way you build up Keyhole Ken. If you do this quickly it can give a nice loose effect.

4   DRAW THE IMAGE AS A CHILD MIGHT DRAW IT

5   TRY AND "SEE" THE OBJECT ON THE PAPER, THEN SKETCH IT IN

Can you "SEE" a shark here, chasing the fish?

6   KEEP DOODLING

Make an attempt at the image, then keep tracing over it and change various parts until it takes the shape you want. Be loose and quick to begin with. Very often the first doodle will be the best one.

Doodle ...   trace and alter... until it looks right.

Drawing without picture reference

7   DRAW THE OUTLINE FIRST, THEN FILL IN THE REST

8   ONLY USE A PART OF THE OBJECT OR FIND AN EASIER ANGLE

9   BE EXTREMELY LOOSE AND SKETCHY

10 DRAW IMPORTANT POINTS OF REFERENCE FIRST

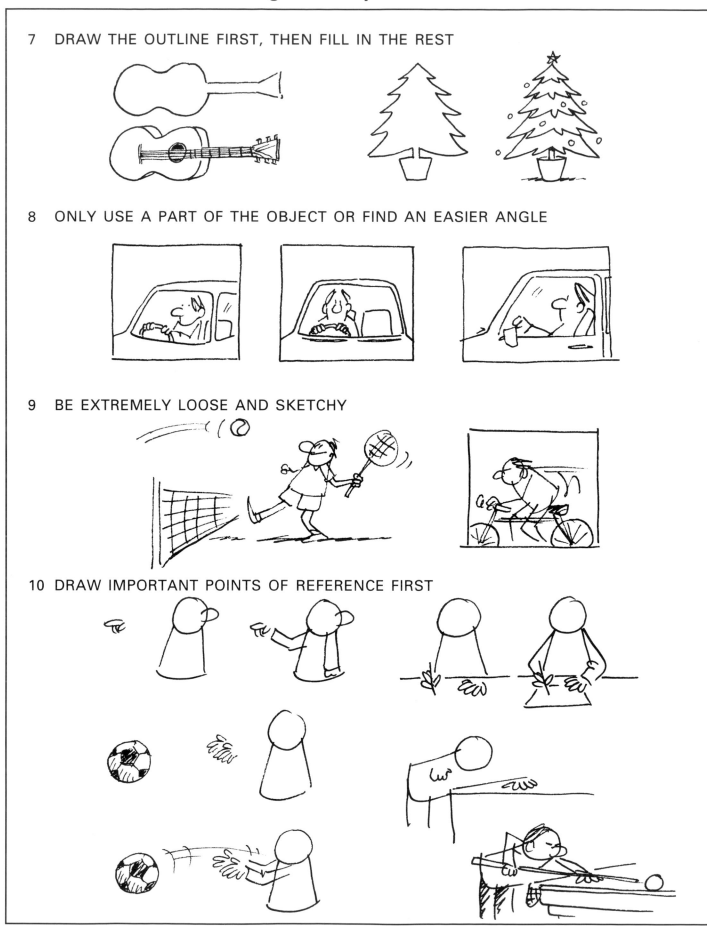

11 BE YOUR OWN MODEL FOR DIFFICULT POSES

For instance, if you wanted to draw someone kicking a ball, stand up, pose yourself in the position and then take each part of your body a step at a time. Check the angle of your upper body – then DRAW IT. Pose again in the same position, Check the angle of one of your legs – then DRAW IT. Pose again, and so on . . .

back angled

leg bent, foot centred

other leg bent, thigh horizontal

left arm angled down and bent

etc.

12 USE A MIRROR FOR DIFFICULT EXPRESSIONS OR HAND POSITIONS

13 GET SOMEONE ELSE TO POSE AND DO A QUICK SKETCH

CAN I SCRATCH MY NOSE?

NO!

14 IF YOU RUN INTO DIFFICULTIES – MAKE A SNACK!

Developing a personal style

It is helpful to develop a unique style but don't make uniqueness your chief concern. Aim to please yourself. If you can draw characters that YOU find funny or intriguing then you will find it easier to come up with gags. Look at other cartoon styles that you enjoy and figure out what you most like about them. Copy to begin with but keep experimenting, mix styles up, exaggerate, be ridiculous! Use the Keyhole Ken process to draw an infinite variety of characters.

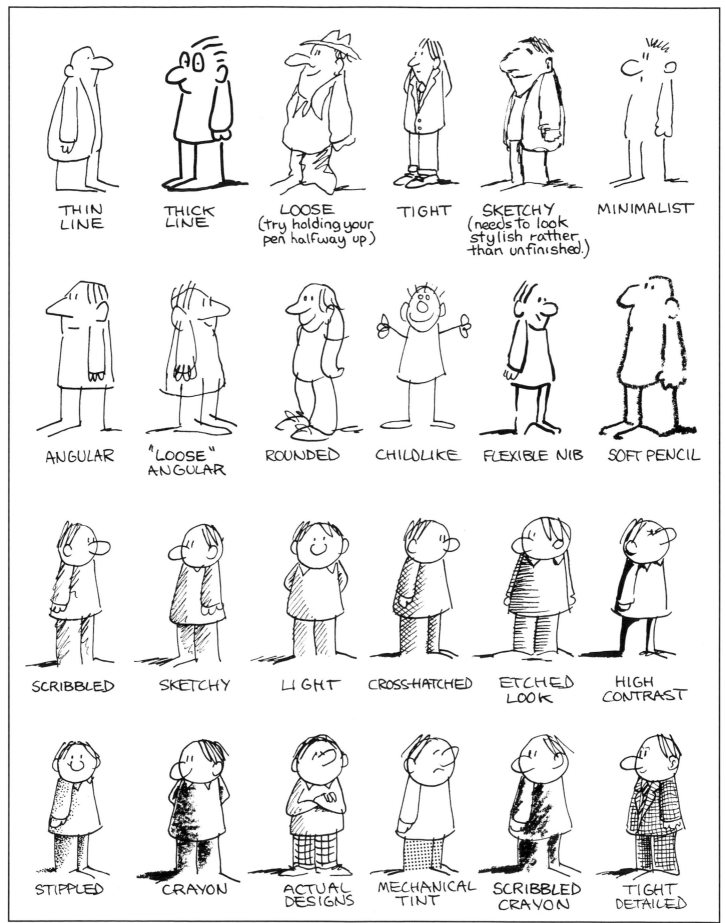

THIN LINE

THICK LINE

LOOSE (try holding your pen halfway up)

TIGHT

SKETCHY (needs to look stylish rather than unfinished.)

MINIMALIST

ANGULAR

"LOOSE" ANGULAR

ROUNDED

CHILDLIKE

FLEXIBLE NIB

SOFT PENCIL

SCRIBBLED

SKETCHY

LIGHT

CROSS-HATCHED

ETCHED LOOK

HIGH CONTRAST

STIPPLED

CRAYON

ACTUAL DESIGNS

MECHANICAL TINT

SCRIBBLED CRAYON

TIGHT DETAILED

Composition

While there are no right or wrong ways to arrange the various elements of a cartoon, there are certain guidelines that beginners can utilize to make their drawings more effective and more interesting.

Let's use the following setup to consider the guidelines.

Ken   a house   a tree   background

1   IS THERE A MOOD YOU WISH TO EXPRESS? This may determine how you lay out the various elements. Think like a film director.

is the house a threatening place?   or a welcoming place?   is Ken nervous?   is it far away?

2   BALANCE (i) Do the elements in your scene fit together on the page or in the panel in an interesting and pleasing way?

too straightforward   a bit cramped   too much blank space   this is more interesting   seek for this balance in all your layouts

BALANCE (ii) Keep important elements grouped together rather than scattered but don't overdo it. Try and link the elements in some way.

too scattered   too tight   more balance

Composition

3   THE CENTER OF ATTENTION To make your drawings more interesting or to direct the reader's attention, EMPHASIZE the more important details of your scene in some way.

when all the elements have the same detail there is no center of interest

in this drawing Ken stands out more

the important element doesn't have to be central

4   DEPTH There are various ways to create a sense of depth.

overlapping

"distance" perspective

"angular" perspective

shading ——— line contrast (as in no.3)

5   SETTING THE SCENE Learn to "set the scene" with a minimum number of objects.

6   BALANCE OF LIGHT AND DARK If you use areas of black or shading remember they are an important part of the composition.

too obvious

more interesting

too little

too much

more balance

Composition

7 Aim for VARIATION in your strip cartoons or comic pages but don't overdo it. Having several panels exactly the same could be part of your "variation." When you rough out a strip or page always consider how the panels work TOGETHER as ONE picture.

bit boring

variation in characters sizes or panel sizes

variation in perspective

variation in black or white areas

variation in poses or expressions

variation in panel borders

Keep in mind that repetitive panels can also be a useful way of conveying feelings of boredom, tension, etc.

8 USE THE BORDERS

this includes us—the viewer   breaking out   these lines border this drawing   extreme close-up   very far away

Exaggeration

Most amateur cartoonists have had some form of art training, which has probably conditioned them to draw what they "see" rather than what they "feel" and so their cartoons often have a lifeless quality. Good cartoons have movement, they "speak" for themselves. If a character is in a rage, smoke comes out of his ears. A character "in love" literally "floats on air." Don't be shy, exaggerate, try to animate your characters, even try and bring your characters' SURROUNDINGS to life.

Perspective – 5 useful rules

1   The farther away an object gets – the smaller it is.

2   The closer an object gets – the bigger it appears.

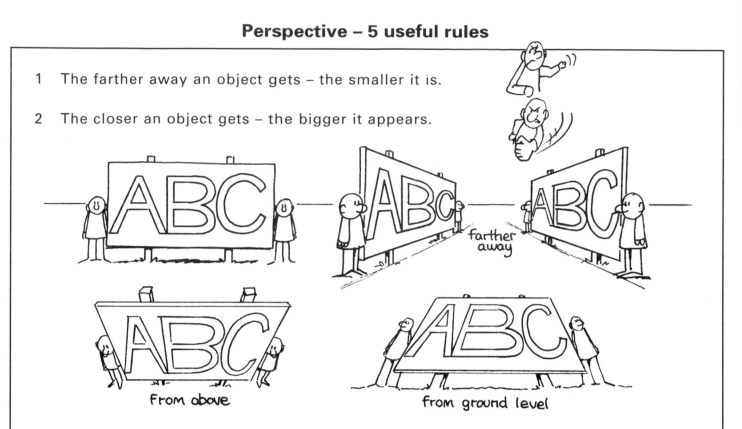

3   HORIZONTAL lines ABOVE your eye level will APPEAR to move DOWNWARDS as they get farther away from you.

4   HORIZONTAL lines BELOW your eye level will APPEAR to move UPWARDS as they get farther away from you.

5   Any horizontal lines that are PARALLEL to each other (running in the same direction) will converge at a point on the horizon called the vanishing point (v.p.).

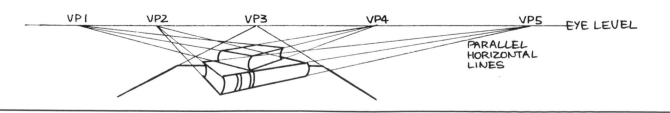

Perspective by instinct

Perspective rules are often best applied AFTER an attempt has been made to place objects INSTINCTIVELY, because very often a cartoon drawing can lose vitality if it is worked out TOO perfectly in the sense of perspective.

For instance, should you want to draw someone standing in a room with lots of pictures on the walls, DON'T make perspective your sole concern. Think about the composition first. Is there a particular mood you wish to convey? Are the pictures overpowering? Is the room big or small? Where are WE viewing the scene from? Are we low down or high up? Do some quick sketches and try to get them *roughly* in perspective.

close up   Far away   from below   from behind

You may find that you are perfectly happy with one of these roughs, but should you wish to be more accurate with the perspective, draw in some "perspective lines" OVER your rough and THEN correct parts of the original rough, though trying not to lose the vitality of the sketch.

Say you pick the view from below..

Imagine where the horizon line is.

Now extend one line that looks correct, to the horizon line

Use that point to draw in other lines that are parallel.

Now use these LINES to correct the rough perspective.

Finally, trace a clean image using a light box.

A more realistic Keyhole Ken

Ken is about 4 head heights tall.

The average person is round about 7½ head heights tall.

For cartoons 5 head heights are best.

This makes the basic keyhole shape easy to work out.

often a sweater or jacket line

As well as being taller, the average person is usually thinner than Ken.

Obviously, realistic faces will make a big difference (see next page).

Shoulders will also add to the realism...

Even a neck...

Hands will need to be drawn more realistically.

× ✓

Make the clothing more detailed...

and the body parts more flexible.

Caricatures

To tackle caricatures you first need to learn how to construct a slightly more realistic "basic" face so that you can exaggerate your subject's more prominent features. Use Keyhole Ken as a guide.

Caricatures

By varying the features of these basic face shapes you can come up with some pretty interesting characters. Experiment with added details, such as fuller lips and eyes, double chins, wrinkles, hairstyles, etc.

fuller lips

Fuller eyes

wrinkles

A smile pulls the cheeks up

A frown pulls the cheeks down

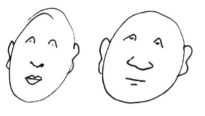

Women's faces are usually thinner with smaller noses.

WAAAAAAAAA!

Caricatures

Now let's use this process to draw caricatures of two very distinctive personalities, Laurel and Hardy. If you are working from a photograph, make a photocopy of it measuring about 3 inches square. Now trace around the main outlines – but don't attempt any shading.

As you build up the caricatures exaggerate the more prominent features.

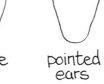

average nose   eyes high up   long face   pointed ears   mouth near nose, distinctive grin, cheek lines   untidy hair

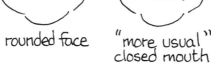

wider nose   slit eyes   rounded face   "more usual" closed mouth   very distinctive hair

close to the tracing   extreme exaggeration

Basic anatomy – the body

Should you wish to draw very realistic cartoons it is helpful to build up the various parts of the body using more workable underlying shapes. Then you can use this framework to draw your final image.

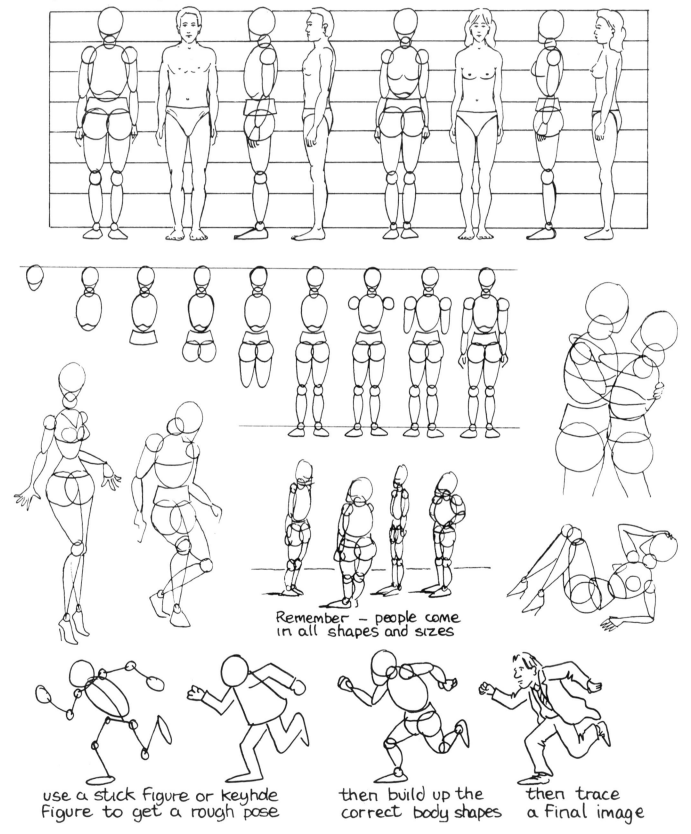

Remember – people come in all shapes and sizes

use a stick figure or keyhole figure to get a rough pose

then build up the correct body shapes

then trace a final image

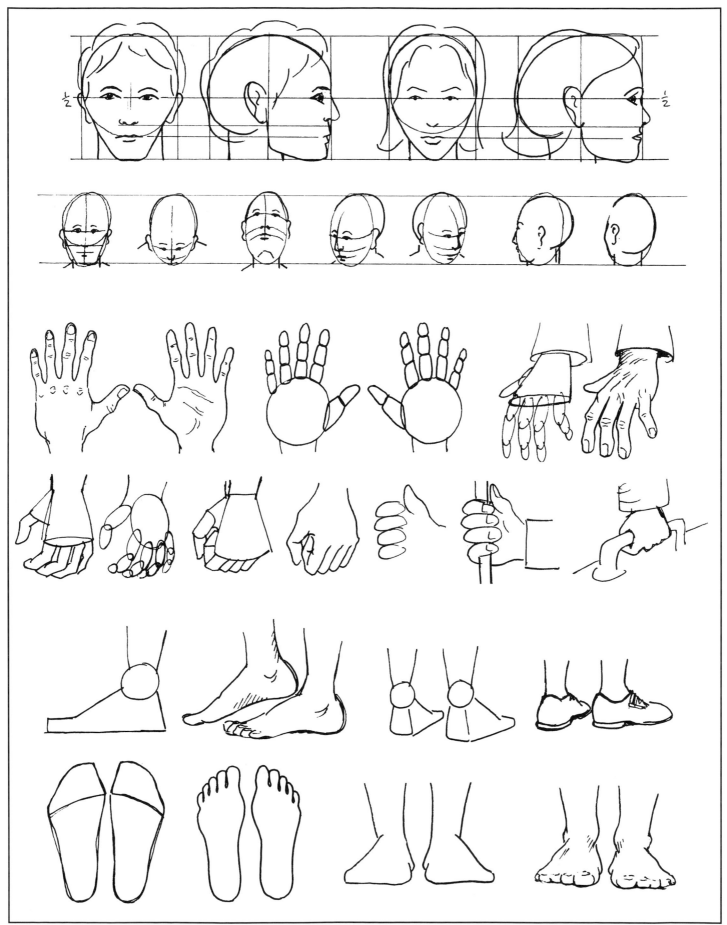

Useful poses

WEIGHT

Useful poses

Useful poses

Cartoon language

Texture and form

soft

sharp

the pull of a button

metallic

fine

coarse

hairy

woolly

sponge

bone

wax

reflective

broken

smoke

creased

stringy

steam

sack

hot

old

new

soiled

54

Texture and form

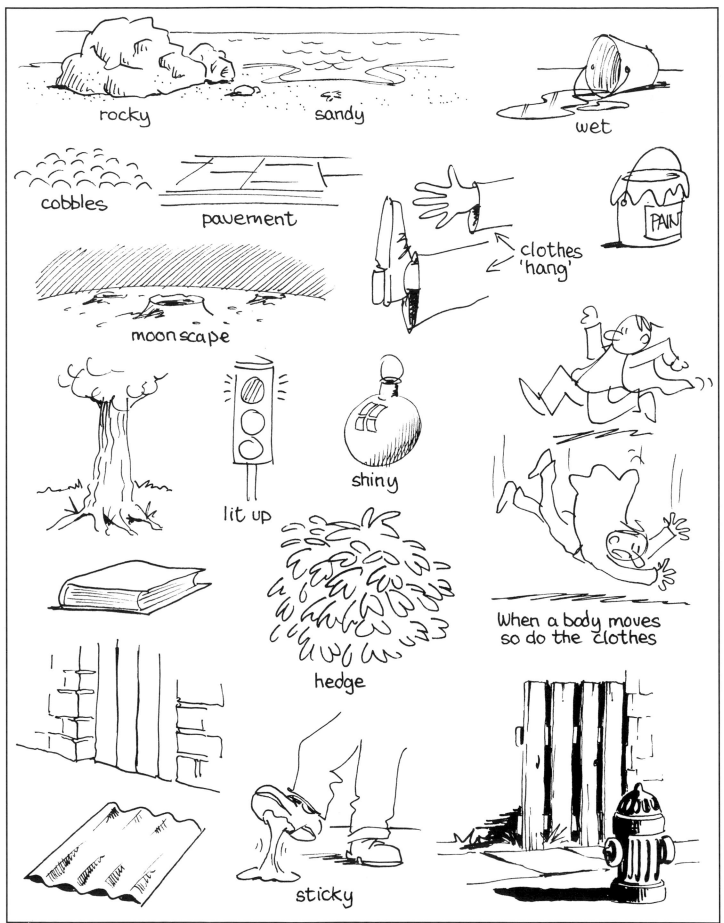

rocky

sandy

wet

cobbles

pavement

clothes 'hang'

PAINT

moonscape

lit up

shiny

book

hedge

When a body moves so do the clothes

sticky

Useful outdoor reference

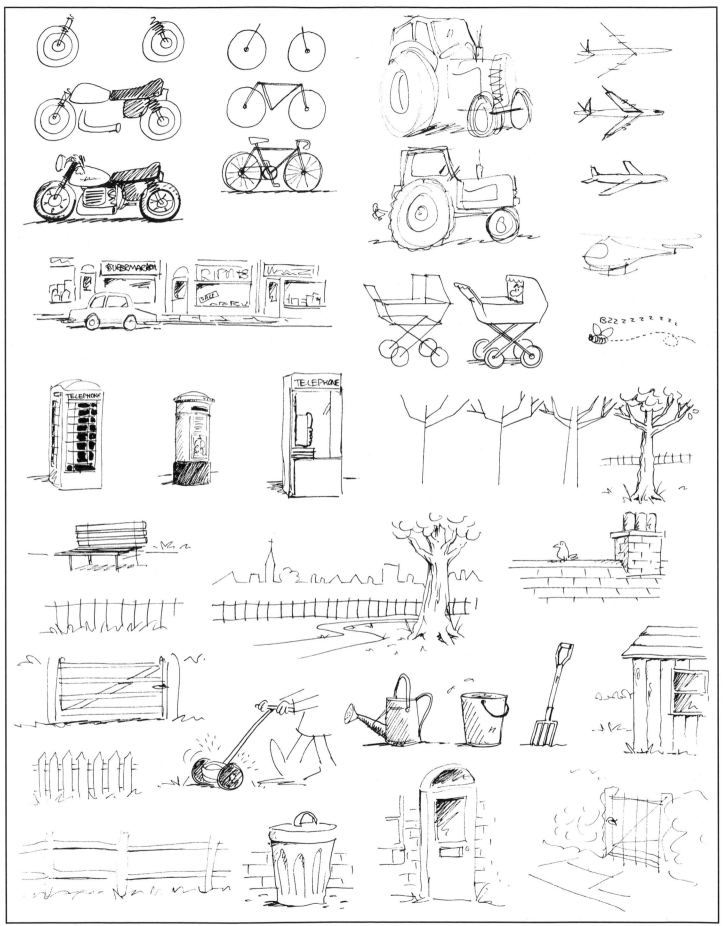

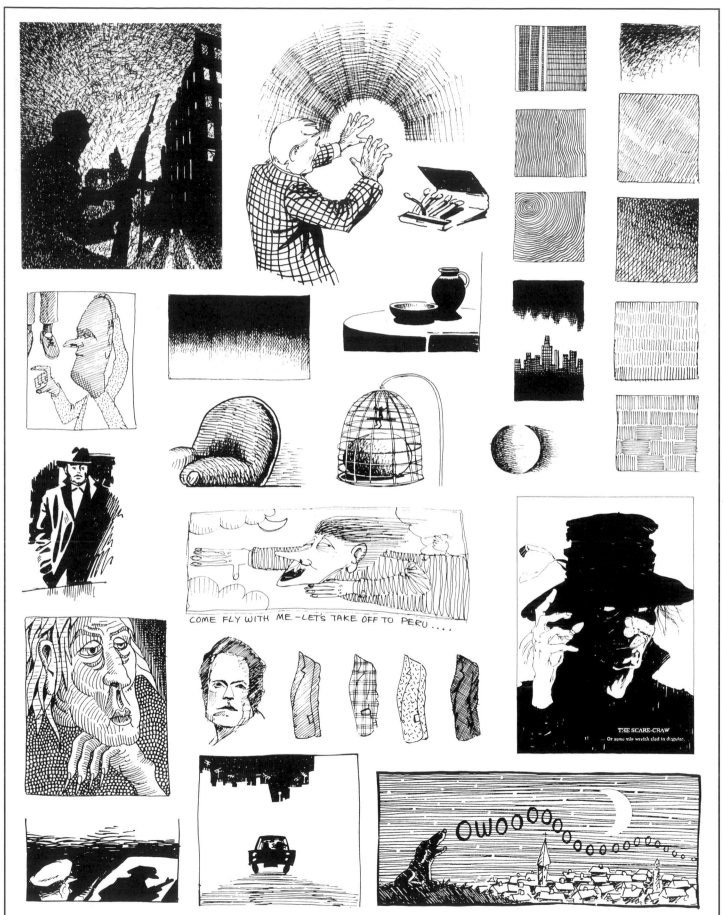

COME FLY WITH ME — LET'S TAKE OFF TO PERU . . . .

THE SCARE-CRAW
Or some vile wretch clad in disguise.

OWOOOOOOOOOOOoooo

Coloring your work

While there are numerous ways to color your cartoons, there is one GUARANTEED way to make your coloring look professional, and that is by using PANTONE* markers.

A lot of cartoons nowadays are computer-colored and markers can give you a similar effect – clean, flat colors (which don't buckle the paper).

Figuring out which ones to use is a process of trial and error. Study other cartoonists' work and decide upon a minimum number of colors that will get you started. But be prepared for a shock when you find out how much they cost!

However, when it comes to coloring body parts, skin-colored markers are not always effective, and I would recommend you use COLORED PENCILS instead.

The process is simple. Apply the markers to good-quality photocopies of your black and white drawings.

Should the black lines bleed under the color, try another copying machine.

Initially use these photocopies to experiment with until you find color combinations which feel harmonious and look professional. You can use your final version as finished artwork.

Once you get the feel for it you soon find that markers are easy to use and enable you to get through a lot of coloring reasonably quickly.

The drawing on the front of this book was colored with markers.

Here are a few shades that I recommend.

Warm Gray	1T	
Warm Gray	3T	very useful as "color shading"
Cool Gray	1T	
Cool Gray	3T	
480 – T	– a good brown for trees, fences, furniture, clothes	
292 – T	– a "blue jeans" color	
375 – T	– grass green	
277 – T	– a light blue sky (the lightest there is, unfortunately)	
679 – T	– a pastel purple color for clothes, settees, beds, etc.	
134 – T	– a sandy yellow color	

Your local art shop may GIVE you a free marker to let you try it out (though invariably it's always the same color).

*The TRIA™ range of PANTONE® (Pantone, Inc's check-standard trademark for color) by Letraset® Color Markers.

The light box

Draw something on a page, and place a clean white sheet of paper on top. You may just barely see the drawing on the bottom page. Now, keeping the pages together, hold them up to a light and you'll see that the image becomes much clearer and could easily be traced (if it wasn't so awkward).

This is how a light box works. It is really just a tracing machine. You can simply place a clean sheet of paper over your quick sketches on the box, turn on the light and trace a more finished, corrected drawing. You can even move the two pages around to better position various elements in your drawings. It is a VERY useful piece of equipment.

Here are some guidelines for constructing your own light box.

I have recommended a good size to make it, but you don't have to stick to this. There are various lengths of fluorescent light fittings. Make sure the glass you use for the top is strong enough to lean on; the frosted perspex doesn't have to be very thick.

NOTE: If you don't know anything about electricity, get someone who does; it can be dangerous!

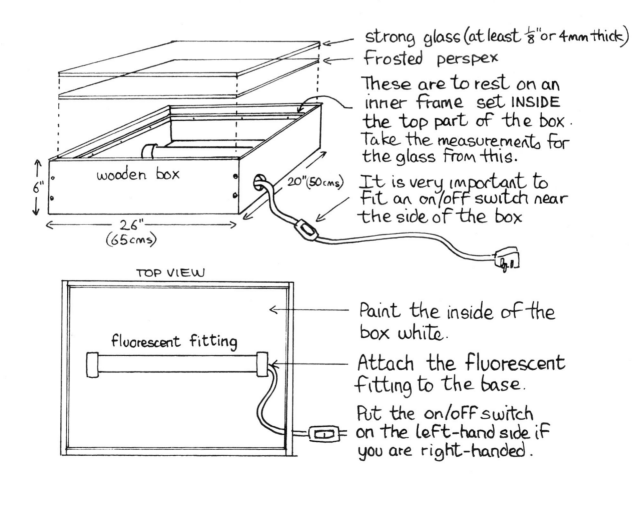

strong glass (at least ⅛" or 4mm thick)

Frosted perspex

These are to rest on an inner frame set INSIDE the top part of the box. Take the measurements for the glass from this.

wooden box

6"

20" (50cms)

It is very important to fit an on/off switch near the side of the box

26" (65cms)

TOP VIEW

fluorescent fitting

Paint the inside of the box white.

Attach the fluorescent fitting to the base.

Put the on/off switch on the left-hand side if you are right-handed.

There is no standard style of lettering for cartoons. Anything goes, even untidy writing could look effective as the "voice" of an untidy character.

If, to begin with, you just want to make your lettering look more "professional," here are a few tips.

Practice writing the alphabet again and again on lined paper. Keep experimenting with the structure of the letters and the spacing.

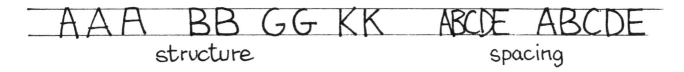

structure   spacing

The letter "S" can be difficult to master. The secret is to make the upper curve SLIGHTLY smaller than the lower one.

Keep practicing until you come up with an alphabet that looks confidently written, evenly balanced and generally pleasing to the eye.

ABCDEFGHIJKLMNOPQRSTUVWXYZ

Try out as many drawing instruments as you can for lettering. You'll only find out through trial and error which are best suited to your abilities and needs.

An easy way to "place" lettering in your cartoon strips is to use a light box. First of all rough out the strip the same size as the finished artwork will be, and try to place the lettering instinctively. From this you can then trace a more accurate "rough," which can then be used in turn to help you draw the finished strip.

Try the lettering in one or two "roughs".

Tidy it up and center it by tracing it on a light box

Use guidelines if you need to.

You don't HAVE to "center" each line.

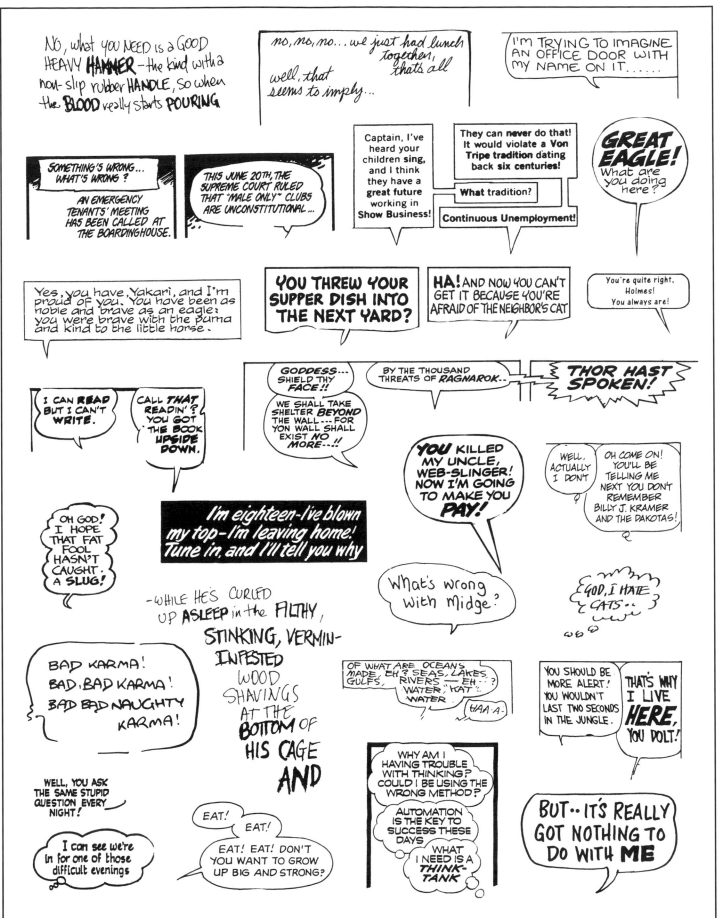

Writing Gags

Writing gags – oiling the machinery

Many people would lead you to believe that the ability to write jokes for cartoons is something you either have or don't have and there's nothing you can do about it. That's NONSENSE! You can learn it like everyone else. It's not EASY, but it GETS easier the more you PRACTICE.

It is obviously best to learn how to DRAW cartoon characters first but while you are doing so there are certain things you can do to prepare yourself for writing jokes.

Now and then try to be VISUALLY humorous with your drawing practice. Just DOODLE. Take things to extremes.

Start drawing cartoons for friends and family – on letters or notes, or make your own birthday and Christmas cards. Just draw out ACTUAL humorous situations you and people around you have been involved in and maybe add a comment or two. Once you start this, people begin to expect it of you which FORCES you to think of more and more ideas. This is an easy introduction to writing gags and people LOVE receiving personal cards like this.

Try and add humorous captions to illustrations or photos in encyclopedias and magazines.

Read as many cartoon books as you can.

Finding a "gag" situation

In Cartoonsville a "one-shot" cartoon is called a "gag."

The first thing you need to find for a gag is a SITUATION. The best source of possible situations is an encyclopedia, preferably one with plenty of illustrations. Just flick through it until something catches your eye and then make a QUICK sketch of whatever it is.

spacemen   cavemen   Nelson

Or you can use typical cartoon situations. Don't hesitate to do this to begin with, but later on try and come up with more original setups.

snake charmer   Flying carpet

Don't discard a possible situation that you come across in a magazine or book just because you can't immediately come up with a great joke for it. SKETCH IT. Der are veys to make ze situation talk!

Let's use the oldest situation in the book to take you through the gag-writing process step by step – the "desert island" scenario. Keep in mind that this process must be studied over a long period of time. Rome wasn't built in a day.

Writing gags – step 1

The first thing you have to do is make a START. Things will not begin to move if you simply sit and stare at your chosen setup.

If you EXPAND on the situation and draw some related images then you obviously have more to work with.

Here are some suggestions – see what you can add to this list.

RELATED IMAGES

- What obvious images can you associate with the situation?
- What OBJECTS could possibly be in the scene?
- What CHARACTERS could possibly be in the scene?
- Imagine you are there. Look around, what ELSE do you see?
- Does the scene remind you of anything?
- Try the scene from far away / close up.
- Try the scene from above or below, what could be above or below?
- Change PARTS of the scene – make them different shapes, sizes, textures; make them bigger, smaller, TOO big, TOO small.
- Add more people, less people, too many people, too few people.
- Change the sex of the characters.
- Change their nationalities.
- Try different age groups – elderly, babies, teenagers.
- Change the setting to daytime, nighttime.
- What effect would the seasons have – spring, summer, autumn, winter?
- Place a TOTALLY unlikely object in the scene.
- Is there some BIG event you could imagine taking place.
- Is there some minor event that could spark a situation?
- What is the biggest OBJECT that could enter the scene?
- What is the smallest OBJECT that could enter the scene?
- _____
- _____
- _____
- _____
- _____
- _____
- _____
- _____

Now try a few of the above suggestions on some of the NEW images you've drawn. You should have plenty.

Related images – example sketches

Writing gags : step 2 – wider observations

- What is the TOTAL exaggeration of the situation?
- What would your favorite cartoonists do with the scene?
- Begin a conversation between the characters – ANYTHING at all. See where it leads you.
- Set the scene in the Past or the Future – from BC to 2020.
- Is there a well-known saying or expression about the situation you could incorporate or adapt?
- What feature of the character(s) could be relevant?
- Totally change the props in the scene – be ridiculous.
- Relate the characters' USUAL situation to something else.
- What else could the characters possess, something that might seem unimportant, but which might spark off a situation?
- Show the character – as a child / at home / on the toilet / in the supermarket / at a movie / restaurant / dentist, etc.
- Imagine different scenarios – why, for example, would people be fleeing for their lives in the scene?
- Why would the police or fire brigade be there?
- Is it an historical event?
- What would a complete twit say (like Stan Laurel)?
- Does ANY object in the scene bring to mind ANYTHING else at all that could lead to further images?
- What would a child say to his or her parent about the scene – or vice versa?
- Could it be relevant to modern society or the environment, or be a comment on politics, advertising, war, capitalism, poverty?
- What would be REALLY sick (though tone this down to something acceptable)?
- What could these people have to say – a child, a tourist, a crowd of onlookers, a police detective, an alien, an animal, Rod Serling, a TV reporter, a neighbor, a mother, father, pet, husband, wife?

Could any of these characteristics spark off an idea?

Laughing, mad, crying, bored, hungry, nervous, terrified, sad, dead, rich, poor, scruffy, tidy, bigoted, stupid, envious, in agony, sleepy, insomniac, bad-tempered, passionate, brave, scared, drunk, in love, sarcastic, embarrassed, henpecked, annoying, overtalkative, smelly, clumsy, walking disaster, brokenhearted, sulking, fashionable, very weird, hypercritical, boastful, argumentative, excited, impatient, hysterical, fussy, nosey, fanatical, dictatorial, artistic, musical, scientific, lonely, reclusive, famous, infamous, pathetic . . .

Writing gags : step 3 — "problem" method

Cartoons can hold a mirror up to life and very often they can remind us that it's possible to laugh at some of our problems and thereby work through them. Or we can laugh at the man on the desert island because perhaps WE feel isolated sometimes and it's nice to have some company. Maybe we just laugh because we're glad someone is worse off than ourselves.

Gags are often based on the fact that some "problem" exists. Not necessarily serious problems, just some reason why what was meant to happen can't or didn't happen.

It helps to look at your images and ask yourself –

• What is MEANT to happen – what could PREVENT this?

• Why do the characters not get along with each other?

• What drama could occur to spark off a humorous situation?

• What could go wrong with the events? (As in Laurel and Hardy films.)

• Could some PART of the scene cause a "problem"?

• Imagine you are one of the characters – whom would you LEAST want to be with or meet in this situation?

EXAMPLES

Throws 'message in a bottle' which is supposed to reach civilization – WHAT PREVENTS THIS?

Reaches the island., Can't get on – WHY NOT?

They don't get along with each other WHY?

Apart from being a castaway what ELSE can go wrong?

Writing gags : experimental doodling – examples

Just draw anything that comes to mind.

sends for a boat

Christmas Island ?

coconuts

Been here long ?

QUICK SAND

TO THE BEACH

Writing gags – complete method

By this stage you may have come up with some jokes but, if not, keep LOOKING, keep experimenting. Be quick, just do loose sketches. If a drawing seems to have possibilities expand on it again using the 3 methods. The whole point is to set your mind FLOWING in the right direction so that something amusing will pop into it.

Gag situations

Deep sea diver

Hairdressers

Concert Pianist

Cook

Vet

Eye test

Surgeons

Magicians

Doctors /Dentists

Radioactivity

$E = MC^2 + 2\frac{1}{2}$

Scientists

Psychiatrist

Metal Detector

First dog in space

Big telescope

CARTOON STRIPS These differ from "one-shot" gags in two fundamental ways. First, instead of having the humorous situation confined to a single drawing, you can develop across a series of frames, with the "punch line" appearing in the final one. Second, the characters who appear in the strip are normally the same ones brought together in subsequent strips – indeed, for as long as the cartoonist can keep creating humorous situations for them. This repetitiveness allows the development of the characters' personalities in a way not possible in gags.

The first consideration in creating a workable cartoon strip is to figure out a location or "setup" and then gather up a suitable cast of characters.

You could drive yourself mad by trying to be TOO original to begin with because everything SEEMS to have been done. If you have a great idea for a cat or a dog, don't scrap it just because of Garfield and Snoopy. It's a big world, and there's plenty of room for more funny cartoon cats and dogs.

Endeavor to be as original as you can but try and let it happen – don't force it. Start drawing characters that appeal to you and see where it leads. The important thing is to get STARTED. After a while you'll begin to understand how it all works and THEN you'll get ideas for more original setups.

A lot of beginners worry about the size that they should draw a cartoon strip. The best thing to do is to draw the characters at whatever size is most comfortable for you and THEN use this as a guide to working out your panel measurements. A lot will also depend on what type of drawing instrument you use. There are no fixed rules. Keep experimenting until you FEEL happy with your artwork.

At the very beginning, don't worry too much about panel sizes or about the pens and paper you should use. All that does is give you an excuse not to work on the important stuff – the drawing and the jokes. Just DRAW, DRAW, DRAW. And STUDY the joke-making process. In finding a location or setup and a cast of characters it is helpful (if you don't go for a "family" strip) to look through encyclopedias, which have tons of images that might help spark something.

Remember, don't give up if the world's most original idea doesn't hit you in the face. Just draw away – experiment – try ANY set of characters (from just a few to a whole town if you wish!) to see how it works. Treat all this as necessary practice. We can learn much from our mistakes.

The opposite page gives you an idea of the "complete" process you can go through to create a cartoon strip. It is much like the process used for GAGS with some other things you have to take into consideration.

The pages following go into it all in more detail.

Cartoon strips – the complete process

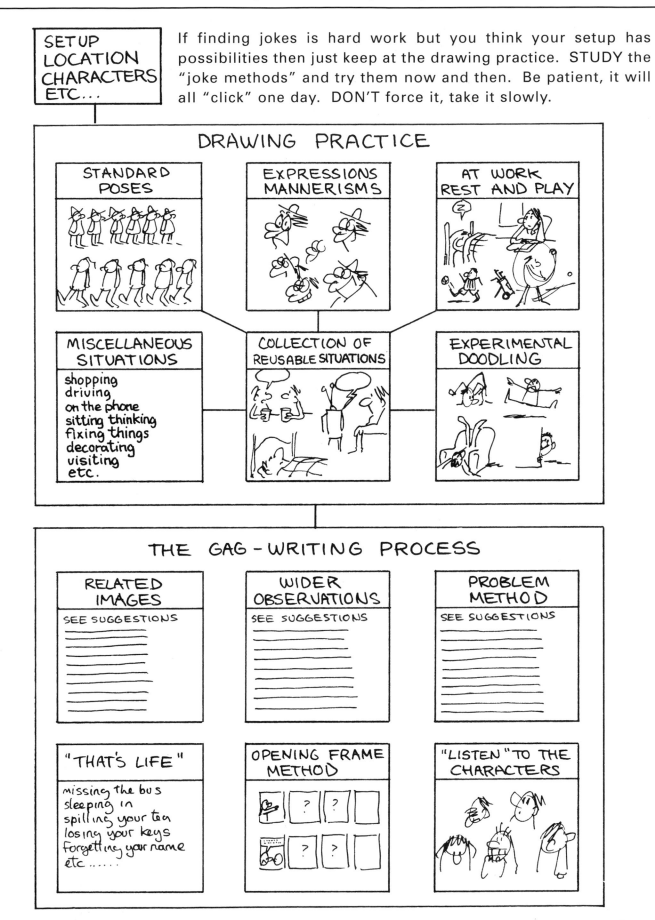

SETUP
LOCATION
CHARACTERS
ETC...

If finding jokes is hard work but you think your setup has possibilities then just keep at the drawing practice. STUDY the "joke methods" and try them now and then. Be patient, it will all "click" one day. DON'T force it, take it slowly.

DRAWING PRACTICE

STANDARD POSES

EXPRESSIONS MANNERISMS

AT WORK REST AND PLAY

MISCELLANEOUS SITUATIONS

shopping
driving
on the phone
sitting thinking
fixing things
decorating
visiting
etc.

COLLECTION OF REUSABLE SITUATIONS

EXPERIMENTAL DOODLING

THE GAG-WRITING PROCESS

RELATED IMAGES

SEE SUGGESTIONS

WIDER OBSERVATIONS

SEE SUGGESTIONS

PROBLEM METHOD

SEE SUGGESTIONS

"THAT'S LIFE"

missing the bus
sleeping in
spilling your tea
losing your keys
forgetting your name
etc......

OPENING FRAME METHOD

"LISTEN" TO THE CHARACTERS

Cartoon strips – drawing practice

STANDARD POSES

If you have a fair idea for a cast of characters, then start to practice drawing them over and over again so that they always look like the SAME characters. This is VITALLY important for a cartoon strip and gets you started without wondering what to do!

EXPRESSIONS AND MANNERISMS

When you get to know a set of characters by repeatedly drawing them, it is very useful to let THEM carry out humorous conversations while you kind of "listen in" and write them down. I know that sounds daft but it does happen. By changing the expressions and mannerisms, you can "overhear" new conversations whenever you want.

"I've got it!"   "Nag, nag, nag."   "Oh, please God."   "That's a laugh."

AT WORK, REST AND PLAY

The cartoon strips that work best are usually the ones that hold up a mirror to modern society and deal with things we are ALL familiar with, namely the things we do at work, rest and play. Draw these situations regularly and use personal experiences.

Cartoon strips – drawing practice

MISCELLANEOUS SITUATIONS

There are a million and one things you might miss when you think generally in terms of work, rest and play. Things that are still familiar to all of us.

Shopping, getting the bus, driving, at the vet's, sitting thinking, fixing things, decorating, visiting people, etc.

Make up your own list and draw scenes from some of them.

EXPERIMENTAL DOODLING

Very often, just drawing your characters in funny poses or in certain settings or costumes or whatever, can help you "see" a joke. If nothing else is working, just DOODLE – experiment – be loose and exaggerate a lot. Put your characters in unlikely poses and see what happens.

COLLECTION OF "REUSABLE" SITUATIONS

The more you practice drawing your characters, the more you will see certain situations that could be used again and again to get jokes. It's a good idea to collect these into one folder so that you can go through it from time to time. These situations can be handy if your "brain" dries up.

RELATED IMAGES (see the suggestions on page 68)

This is basically the same process as for "one-shot" GAGS but this time you need to keep the related images within the bounds of your setup.

WIDER OBSERVATIONS (see the suggestions on page 70)

Again, you cannot stray too far away from your setup but DO experiment. Always be open to changes and new directions.

The list of characteristics on page 70 can be VERY useful in a cartoon strip. For instance you might decide to have one of your characters crying – so WHY is he crying, WHAT problem has occurred to make him cry? Etc., etc. This helps your mind begin to work. Always sketch ideas – no matter how daft they may at first seem. The SKETCH may help you see a really clever idea.

PROBLEM METHOD (see page 72)

The best way to understand how this method works is to study other cartoon strips and work "backwards" to see how the theme was developed. Then ask yourself how the strip COULD have started off using your idea of a "problem." These problems don't have to be major or serious, just humorous alterations of what was meant to happen in the normal run of events.

For instance, asking yourself "WHY can't character "A" get out of bed?" is more helpful than just staring at a drawing of that character lying in bed. The aim is to expand on every situation to start your creativity flowing.

THAT'S LIFE SITUATIONS (personal experiences)

You know the ones: the missing keys – oversleeping – missing the bus – forgetting someone's name – "putting your foot in it" – spilling your carefully prepared snack all over the floor - finally finding a need for something you threw out yesterday – etc. There are a million scenarios with humorous potential right under your nose.

Cartoon strips – the gag-writing process

OPENING FRAME METHOD

As mentioned before, sometimes we need to give our mind a kick start before a joke will pop into it. This opening frame method is often very useful for this. Simply mark out two to four panels and draw ANY situation involving your characters in the first panel and then see if any ideas come to mind regarding the complete strip.

You could also make your character SAY something – ANYTHING at all, and see what happens from that. Experiment, draw out LOTS of three or four panel strips and draw something in each opening panel.

LISTEN TO THE CHARACTERS

Your characters will take on a life of their own once you get a few jokes under your belt. This will give you a direction to go in. The characters will come to life more, and more jokes will follow and so it will build up and become easier. But it takes TIME, so be patient. I doubt if anyone has created a successful cartoon strip overnight.

Whatever happens – don't ever take it all too seriously or it will show in your cartoons. Work hard, but if it's becoming a chore, STOP for a while – wait until you feel in the mood again. If you try to force it you could waste MORE time in the long run. Our minds still work on things even when we are not consciously thinking about them. Let this natural process take place. Relax, have fun.

A cartoon strip from start to finish

After you have a character or set of characters and have got to know them better by drawing them a lot while imagining their personalities, here's one way you could tackle an actual strip.

PICK A SITUATION I draw a character called Conrad who sleeps all day. Let's say I was going to work an idea out for him. I might first of all draw him in his favorite place – bed.

EXPAND ON THE SITUATION From this drawing I would then find as many related images as possible, as I suggested before. For instance, what objects are in the room? There is a clock, a bed, a window, bedclothes, etc. Think of a situation for each item. Does the clock go off? Why would this shock him? Why would it be a problem? Is the bed uncomfortable? Is he thinking about how much he loves the bed? What is outside the window? A window cleaner? A bird chirping? Noisy workmen? How do these things affect him? Have his bedclothes got a cartoon design on them? Is he cold or warm? What else can happen to him because he is in bed? Does someone call? Does he have to get up? WOULD he get up? What is he thinking about? Is he dreaming or having a nightmare? Is there a big spider hanging down from the ceiling, etc?

Quickly draw lots of related images and then expand on each situation again if you need to. Always keep in mind your characters' personalities. How would they react to certain things? Are they sarcastic, lazy, scared, silly...? LOOK at your drawings and LISTEN to your characters as if they were acting out their roles in the world you have set them in. Don't forget to draw various expressions to bring them to life.

A cartoon strip from start to finish

DO A QUICK SKETCH OF YOUR "JOKE". By going through this "related images" process I came up with an idea for a strip where Conrad gets really annoyed about noisy workmen outside in the street. I then sketched the basic idea very quickly.

DO A MORE FINISHED ROUGH Usually these quick sketches have nice spontaneous elements that are worth keeping. Also, from them you can tell if certain panels need to be made bigger or smaller, because of the scene or the amount of dialogue. After taking all this into consideration you could try a few more quick rough sketches and then draw up a more finished rough, the same size as the final artwork will be. When doing this, fit the dialogue in first and build the drawings around that.

COMPLETE THE FINAL ARTWORK Your final artwork can now be drawn onto artboard, using your "finished rough" as a guide. Or you could trace a finished drawing from your rough onto paper, using a light box. If you make any mistakes, don't do the whole strip again, just draw the correction on another piece of paper, cut it out and paste it in.

Little Town Blues By HALL

Gag situations

On the street

Street artist

Statue

TELEPHONE

I SPEAK YOUR WEIGHT

BUS STOP

MEN AT WORK

QUEUE HERE

SALE

Gossips

Back of crowd

?

MAIL

FLAGS

NEWS

Tramp

THE END IS

Gag situations

Gag situations

Decorating

Home movies

Bird table

Ironing

Playpen

I'M LEAVING YOU THELMA

Clothes line

Courting

Sleep walker

Bedtime story

Man in wardrobe

Woken up

Gag situations

87

Gag situations

"ELEMENTARY MY DEAR WATSON"

Little Red Riding Hood

Robinson Crusoe

Genie

Zorro

Jack and the beanstalk

Robin Hood

Dr Frankenstein

Angry mob

Humpty Dumpty

The Mummy

Rip Van Winkle

Archaeologists

Superman

Pied Piper

Graveyard

Hell

Ghosts

Count Dracula

Death

Gag situations

Firing squad

Road sweeper

Monk

Sheep shearer

Firemen

PATENTS OFFICE

Fortune teller

Museum statues

Potter's wheel

Climbers

Rock band

Sculptor

Awards

Massive crowd

Press Conference

Theatrical agent

AGENT

Gag situations

Gag situations

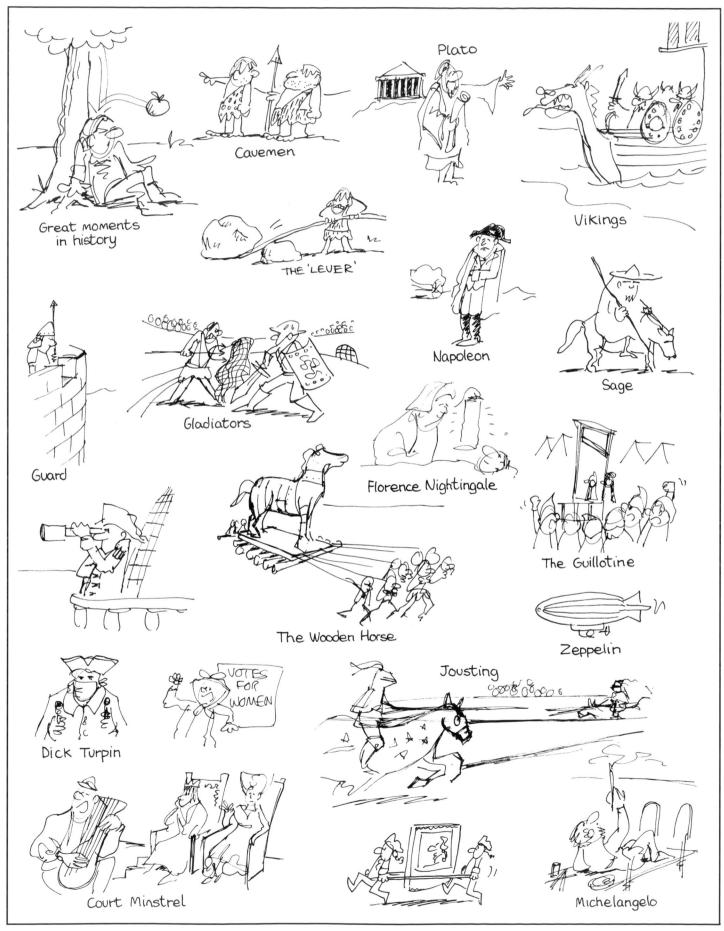

Gag situations

SALOON

The Lone Ranger
and Tonto

Peace pipe

SHERIFF

Cowboys campfire

Rain dance

Davy Crockett

Siesta

Hunter

CASHIER

Stick-up

WANTED

Rodeo

Police

Prison visit

Good cop - Bad cop

Police lineup

Hard Labor

Gag situations

Trick cyclist

Sky divers

Juggling

Darts

The beam

Sack race

Jogging

Pole vaulter

Relay race

Hurdles

Jury

Skater

Tug of war

94

Gag situations

Presentation and Selling

The cartoon markets

Before you submit ANY cartoons, try them out on family and friends. Give due consideration to any criticism and be prepared to work on it even if you think it is undeserved. So much effort goes into our first cartoons we often convince ourselves they are better than they really are. Be suspicious of your early work. Keep improving on it. I had to do this for 5 YEARS before my work was good enough to send out. I hope that this book will help you on your way more quickly than that.

NEWSPAPERS

DAILY STRIPS First try newspapers that have no strips too similar to your own, but make sure your humor will "fit in." The so-called "intellectual" papers WON'T go for a "slapstick" humor strip but the "tabloids" may go for an "intellectual" strip (such as "Peanuts").

National newspapers pay well, regional newspapers don't (because they can use well-known syndicated strips at little cost). In the UK there are a limited number of nationals and most have their full quota of strips – but keep trying, new strips DO appear from time to time. In America of course the market is much bigger and the usual way to break into it is through a syndicate which can afford to send your work out to hundreds (maybe thousands) of papers. However, many cartoonists DO syndicate their own strips successfully.

DAILY PANELS These are single panel cartoons that always appear under a set title. They are generally linked by regular characters, e.g. "Ziggy" by Tom Wilson, or by the style of humor, e.g. "The Far Side" by Gary Larson. Bundles of panel gags are probably stacked high in every editor's office at the moment. If you have some, they had better be good.

WEEKLY STRIPS/PANELS Some newspapers run weekly strips that are relevant to particular weekly features, i.e. TV, fashion, sports, movies, etc. Check a variety of newspapers frequently for possible openings.

GAGS Selling "one-shot" gags is a tough business. They are often seen as mere page fillers by editors and readers alike. If you can get yourself established as a gag cartoonist you will be okay; it's making the breakthrough that's difficult, as most editors stick to their usual cartoonists like glue. The biggest problem is that you can easily get your best work rejected which can affect your confidence. Be prepared to try, try and try again if you want to be a gag cartoonist.

TOPICAL/POLITICAL GAGS You need to know your stuff if you want to do one of these every day. Prove your ability to the editor by sending a topical gag every day for a few weeks.

MAGAZINES

Magazines take the full range of cartoon formats including cartoon illustrations. Several books will tell you which ones take GAGS but the chances are that ANY magazine could take a strip or panel if it was thought good enough. Most magazines (except the satirical ones) will run only ONE STRIP but they may also go for a feature panel or some illustrative cartoons. Submit your work first to the magazines you'd LIKE to appear in if they seem to offer a possible opening, and then try all the rest. Let them keep your work on file.

Specialist magazines such as *Computer Weekly* or *Golf Monthly* can be a good market to explore since they receive fewer submissions than satirical magazines. Don't forget about the weekend newspaper magazines.

Little Town Blues (daily)

gags

"I'm afraid you're badly overdrawn, Mr. Henson."

THINGUMAJIGS (weekly/monthly)

Birdland.. (specialist periodical)

political caricature

(topical)

Behind The Screens..

THE UMPIRE STRIKES BACK

(weekly feature panel)

The markets

COMICS Some comics use strips and gags but if you are interested in full-page stories, then be sure you have plenty of ideas and can meet a deadline. Send some "fashionable" ideas and some more original, experimental ideas if you have them. Send some of your best rough work as well.

GREETING CARDS Many books have a list of greeting card companies or you can find them on the back of cards in the stores. As well as actually making up some of your card ideas, send samples of ALL your work.

ADVERTISING AND DESIGN AGENCIES Designers regularly use free-lance cartoonists and illustrators. Take in a portfolio or mail copies of your work to as many agencies as you can. Always give them something to keep on file.

CARTOON BOOKS Check out this market by spending an hour in a leading bookstore. Forget strip-compilation books, look at "one-shot" books about cats or dogs or Father's Day or the "series" cartoon books (e.g. "The Duffer's Guide to . . ."). Most cartoon books are based on one theme.

ILLUSTRATIONS FOR BOOKS Children's books are obviously a good market for the cartoonist. If you aren't a natural storyteller, team up with a writer. Several books have more advice on this and a comprehensive list of publishers.

There are many different books that use cartoons to illustrate the text or the cover. Get in touch with some local publishers.

OTHER MARKETS Cartoons are used everywhere, from brochures to store signs. Look around, you may find a market that no one else has exploited. Make up lots of inexpensive folders of your work and leave them with anyone you think might need a cartoon for something – shops, printers, sign makers, publishers, trophy shops, T-shirt stores.

SYNDICATES/AGENTS In America, the majority of comic strips are distributed by syndicates. In the UK, because there are only a handful of national newspapers, it is worthwhile submitting your work directly to them. Also, in the UK several newspapers syndicate their own strips, so they may prefer not to use other agencies.

However, you may still wish to try and place your work in the hands of an agent, because they can provide a personal selling service, something you might find unrealistic to have to undertake yourself. They could be on a first-name basis with many editors and will (if you are lucky) keep pushing your work. The very fact that an agent has taken on your work may add some weight to its "worthiness." And, of course, an agent can help sell your work on the international market.

Don't be afraid to telephone various agents and ask for information – about how many newspapers they deal with, what strips they handle and how much commission they take.

cartoon books

business cards

book or magazine illustrations

signs

book covers

greeting cards

advertising and design

T shirts

fax pages

Framed cartoons

animation

Presenting your work

How you present your works says a lot about you. At the end of they day it is the QUALITY of the work that counts, but if your (brilliant) cartoons are poorly presented they may be tossed aside and not even looked at.

GAGS

Gags are normally submitted 5 or 6 at a time on separate sheets of paper. Write your name and address on the back of each one. (If one is accepted, the editor will hold on to it and send the rest back.) For black-and-white work good dark photocopies will do fine but for color work you may have to send the original artwork or hand-colored copies (see page 59). Most publications will typeset the caption for you. Write any captions about 2 inches underneath the gags in pencil. Write them out EXACTLY the way you wish them to appear, with regard to grammar or the use of capitals.

Send the gags with a very brief covering letter and a s.a.s.e. Print all addresses clearly and with as much style as you can (nothing fancy – just stylish).

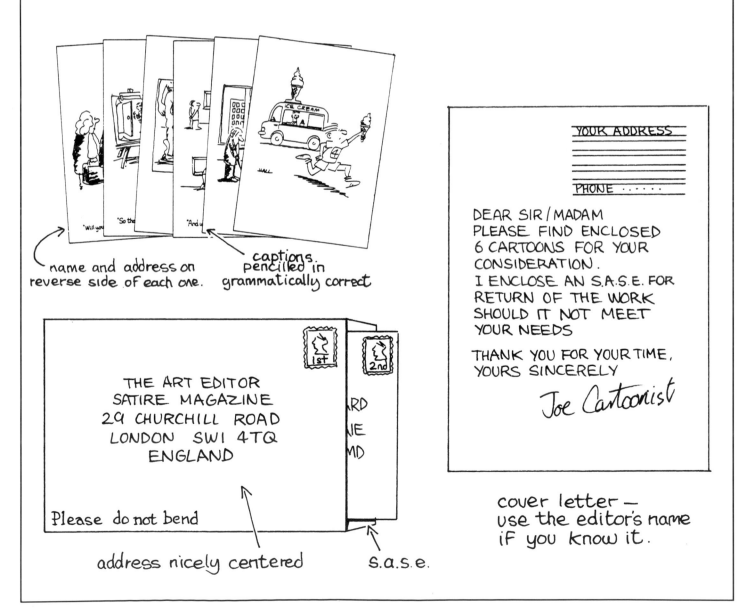

name and address on reverse side of each one.

captions pencilled in grammatically correct

YOUR ADDRESS

PHONE . . . . . .

DEAR SIR / MADAM
PLEASE FIND ENCLOSED
6 CARTOONS FOR YOUR
CONSIDERATION.
I ENCLOSE AN S.A.S.E. FOR
RETURN OF THE WORK
SHOULD IT NOT MEET
YOUR NEEDS

THANK YOU FOR YOUR TIME,
YOURS SINCERELY
Joe Cartoonist

THE ART EDITOR
SATIRE MAGAZINE
29 CHURCHILL ROAD
LONDON SW1 4TQ
ENGLAND

Please do not bend

cover letter –
use the editor's name
if you know it.

address nicely centered

s.a.s.e.

STRIPS / PANELS

Send as many samples as YOU think are necessary to get your idea fully across. There is no set amount. If you can't make up your mind, then send at least 24 samples of a daily or weekly strip (8 pages with 3 strips per page, or 6 pages with 4 strips per page) along with one or two "character" sheets (a page of drawings of each of your characters with a brief description of their personalities).

For a monthly strip send at least 12 (a year's supply) but use 3 per page rather than 4. If possible, include plenty of other examples of your work.

If you use plastic pocket pages, try not to leave any empty. Even fill the space with enlargements of your best character drawings.

Make sure you include some color samples as well and if it's a daily strip you may need to include some colored Sunday strips.

If you want your work back enclose a s.a.s.e. but I would suggest you ask that your work be filed for future consideration. Who knows, the editor may need a new cartoon NEXT month.

Instead of sitting around promising to get a presentation folder together, draw up a rough plan of what needs to be included in it, pin this up and work through it.

AN EXAMPLE OF A WORKSHEET

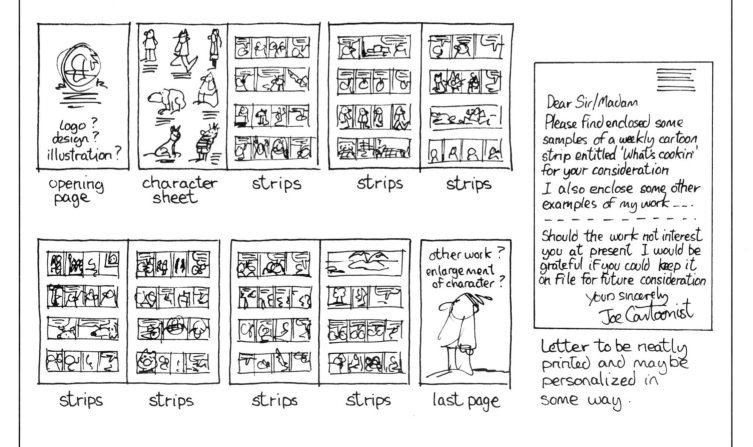

opening page · character sheet · strips · strips · strips

strips · strips · strips · strips · last page

Dear Sir/Madam
Please find enclosed some samples of a weekly cartoon strip entitled 'What's cookin' for your consideration
I also enclose some other examples of my work ___
_ _ _ _ _ _ _ _ _ _ _
Should the work not interest you at present I would be grateful if you could keep it on file for future consideration
yours sincerely
Joe Cartoonist

Letter to be neatly printed and maybe personalized in some way.

PERSONALIZE YOUR SUBMISSIONS IN SOME WAY

It's always a good idea to add a personal touch when submitting your work. Perhaps a cartoon on the letter or some sort of logo that incorporates your name, address and telephone number. Or perhaps a logo on a personal card (which you can enlarge for use on portfolio covers). Spend a LOT of time figuring this out. I won't suggest any ideas because there is no set way that this should be done; it could be ANYTHING as long as it is SUBTLE and personal to you.

PREPARING A PORTFOLIO

If you intend to submit your work in person, then it doesn't really matter what size portfolio you use as long as it is presentable. Always bring along some copies of your work in a folder to leave for filing purposes.

If you are submitting by mail, make sure all your work is presentable and either drawn on, or attached to, standard-size pages. Don't send massive drawings that are awkward to file. If you have a LOT of work to send, use a display book that contains 10 or 20 transparent pockets (you'll find these are cheaper in a big store than an art shop).

Most likely, to begin with, you'll just have 5 to 10 pages to submit, in which case you can put together an inexpensive folder using "loose punched transparent pockets" (as they are called), a sheet of thin cardboard to give support, and a plastic binder to hold them all together.

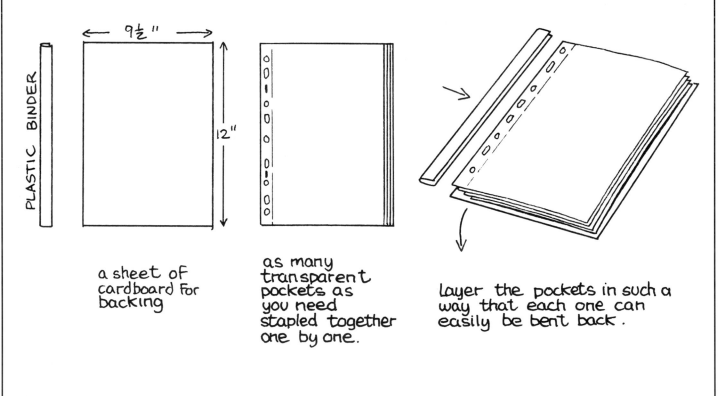

MAKING AN INEXPENSIVE PORTFOLIO

PLASTIC BINDER

9½"

12"

a sheet of cardboard for backing

as many transparent pockets as you need stapled together one by one.

layer the pockets in such a way that each one can easily be bent back.

Presenting your work

PRELIMINARY ENQUIRIES

Should you wish to make a preliminary inquiry of one sort or another, phone and tell whoever answers that you wish to submit some samples of your cartoons or strips, or whatever, and that you'd like to know to whom you should address your submission. This will set the ball rolling and if you have other questions just say, "By the way . . . ." You'll be surprised what you can find out by doing this and it IS a good idea to find out exactly whom to send your work to – it is much more personal.

BEFORE YOU MAIL

Print your name and address on the back of the envelope. Send your work by first-class mail.

HOW LONG SHOULD YOU WAIT FOR A REPLY?

You could take a chance and phone after a week or two to "make sure the work arrived safely." They may tell you there and then if they like it or not, but if they offer no information, don't push it. If you've had no reply after 3 or 4 weeks, phone and politely ask if your work "is still under consideration."

BROADEN YOUR OPTIONS

Gag cartoons should be submitted to only one editor at a time. It is, however, acceptable to submit the same samples of daily, weekly or monthly features to as many editors at one time as you wish. If you are regularly coming up with new ideas, don't be afraid to send them to editors to whom you have previously submitted work. Who knows? You may eventually wear them down.

KEEP A DIARY

It is vitally important to keep a record of EVERY item you send to every publication in case you forget where you've sent what.

COPYRIGHT

In most countries copyright belongs to the person who has drawn or written the work unless it is sold outright. "Gags" need only have your "cartoon signature" on them. For everything else make sure you have a copyright symbol © followed by your name and year. Have a page of these typeset and stick them on your work before you make copies.

REJECTION SLIP BLUES

Don't "expect" rejection slips – always be positive – but should they come don't be dismayed; you can't please all the people all of the time. Maybe the editor wasn't into your type of humor or maybe you DO have a lot of improvements to make to your work. It's all experience. Keep plugging away.

Rejection slip blues

Some advice from King Features Syndicate

KING
FEATURES SYNDICATE

SUBMISSION GUIDELINES

King Features is always happy to look at new comic features for possible syndication. We believe in the art of cartooning and place great importance on looking at new material. Without exception, every comic strip or panel idea submitted to us is carefully considered.

In order to help you present your work in the best possible light and to help us respond to it more quickly, the editors have put together the following questions and answers:

HOW MANY CARTOONS SHOULD I SUBMIT?
Send 24 daily comic strips. It is not necessary to send Sunday comic strips. If we like your daily comics, we will ask to see sample Sunday pages.

WHAT SIZE SHOULD I DRAW MY COMICS?
Most comic strip cartoonists draw their daily comic strips 13" wide x 4" tall. Most single-panel cartoonists draw their daily panel 7" wide by 7" high, not counting the extra space for the caption placed underneath the drawing.

You can draw larger or smaller than that, as long as your cartoons are in proportion to those sizes.

WHAT FORMAT SHOULD I SUBMIT MY CARTOONS IN?
You should reduce your comics to fit onto standard 8-1/2" x 11" sheets of paper. Write your name, address and phone number on each page. Do **not** send your original drawings! Send xeroxes instead.

WHAT ELSE SHOULD I INCLUDE IN THE PACKAGE OF CARTOONS THAT I SEND?
Your total submission package should include:
1) 24 daily comic strips -- on 8-1/2" x 11" paper.
2) A cover letter -- that briefly outlines the overall nature of your comic strip.
3) A character sheet that shows your major characters (if any) along with their names and a paragraph description of each.
4) **A RETURN ENVELOPE WITH YOUR NAME, ADDRESS AND POSTAGE ON IT** -- without a return envelope and postage we usually won't respond to your submission.
5) A resume, samples of previously published cartoons

and other biographical information on your cartooning career would be helpful, but aren't strictly necessary.

WHO SHOULD I SEND MY COMIC FEATURE TO?
Send your cartoons to: Jay Kennedy
Comics Editor
King Features
235 East 45th Street
New York, NY 10017

I AM UNFAMILAR WITH SYNDICATION. CAN YOU EXPLAIN WHAT A CARTOON SYNDICATE DOES?
First, a syndicate decides which comic strips it thinks it can sell best. Then it signs a contract with the cartoonist to create the strip on a regular weekly basis. But most of all, the syndicate edits, packages, promotes, prints, sells and distributes the comic strip to newspapers in the United States and around the world on an ongoing basis.

In short, a syndicate is responsible for bringing the cartoons from the cartoonist to the public.

WHAT DO YOU LOOK FOR IN A SUBMISSION?
We are looking for comic features that will simultaneously appeal to the newspaper editors who buy comics and the newspaper readers whose interest the comic must sustain for years to follow. We don't have a formula for telling us which comics will do that, but we do look for some elements that we believe people respond to.

First, we look for a uniqueness that reflects the cartoonist's own individual slant on the world and humor. If we see that unique slant, we look to see if the cartoonist is turning his or her attention to events that other people can relate to.

Second, we very carefully study a cartoonist's writing ability. Good writing helps weak art, better than good art helps weak writing.

Good art is also important. It is what first attracts readers to a comic strip. We look to see that your art is drawn clearly and with visual impact. We want our comics to be noticed on a page.

Finally, we look for your ability to sustain a high level of quality material. We want comics that readers will enjoy for years and years.

DO I NEED TO COPYRIGHT MY CARTOONS BEFORE SENDING THEM?
No, it's not necessary, but if you feel safer doing so, you can obtain copyright information by contacting the Copyright Office, Library of Congress, Washington, DC 20559.

WHAT ARE MY CHANCES OF GETTING SYNDICATED BY KING FEATURES?
King Features is the largest syndicate. Each year, it gets more than 6,000 submissions of which three are chosen for syndication.

IF I AM A BETTER WRITER THAN AN ARTIST (OR VICE VERSA), WILL THE SYNDICATE MATCH ME UP WITH A PARTNER?
If your work is far enough along that we think it would succeed if only it had a little better art or a little better writing, then the syndicate will attempt to find you a partner. In most cases, however, it is up to the cartoonist to find a partner.

HOW LONG SHOULD I EXPECT TO WAIT BEFORE RECEIVING A REPLY?
We'll make every effort to respond quickly, but at times it may take us as long as six weeks, due to the high volume of submissions we receive.

IF MY COMIC ISN'T ACCEPTED FOR SYNDICATION, CAN YOU STILL CRITIQUE MY WORK?
We receive well over 6,000 submissions a year. As much as we would like to, it is impossible for us to critique all the work we see. Please understand that receiving a form rejection letter from us isn't a negative criticism of your work. It simply means that at the time we saw your work, we didn't feel that newspaper editors would buy your feature.

WHAT ARE THE TERMS OF PAYMENT IF MY WORK IS ACCEPTED?
If your work is accepted for syndication, the proceeds are split 50/50 between the cartoonist and the syndicate. Cartoonists can make between $20,000 and $1,000,000 dollars a year. It all depends on how many newspapers subscribe to your comic strip and how many products are made from your characters.

CAN YOU GIVE ME ANY TIPS TO IMPROVE MY CHANCES OF SUCCESS?
The single best way of improving your chances for success is to practice. Only by drawing and writing cartoons do you get better at it. Invariably the cartoonists whose work we like best turn out to be those who draw cartoons regularly whether anyone sees their work or not.

Another key to success is to read a lot. Read all sorts of things -- fiction, magazines and newspapers. Humor is based on real life. The more you know about life the more you have to write humorously about.

WHAT BOOKS OR MAGAZINES DO YOU RECOMMEND TO HELP ME WITH MY GOAL OF BECOMING A PROFESSIONAL CARTOONIST?
Cartooning - The Art and the Business by Mort Gerberg, published by William Morrow in 1989, gives an excellent overview of the different careers in cartooning.

Cartoonist PROfiles magazine (P.O. Box 325, Fairfield, CT 06430) is a highly informative publication of particular interest if your goal is to become a syndicated newspaper cartoonist.

The Comics Buyer's Guide (700 E. State St., Iola, WI

54990) is a thick weekly newspaper primarily devoted to comic book cartooning, but it does have some coverage of newspaper comics. It is a particularly useful publication for those interested in trading, buying or selling old comics strips and art.

Comics & Sequential Art by Will Eisner, distributed by Eclipse Books (P.O. Box 1099, Forestville, CA 95436), is primarily concerned with the creation of comic books and other longer forms of cartooning, but its technical insights into composition, lettering, anatomy, shading and pacing are useful to all cartoonists.

WHAT ARE SOME OF THE COMMON MISTAKES MADE BY ASPIRING CARTOONISTS?
They often place too much emphasis on coming up with a novel character or setting. A strip starring a giraffe won't get critical acclaim just because there's never been a giraffe strip before. Humor is the most important element of successful comic strips, followed closely by well-defined and interesting characters.

In many cases, aspiring cartoonists develop too narrow a premise. Syndicated comics are meant to last for decades. A cartoon about a character who always falls asleep at the wrong time or talks about just one topic day after day, will quickly get repetitive and boring. Develop characters and situations that will allow you many avenues for humor in the future.

Very few aspiring cartoonists pay enough attention to their lettering. The words need to be lettered neatly enough, _and large enough_, that readers can read them without difficulty.

Newspapers usually print comic strips about 6-1/2" wide. They usually print single panel cartoons 3-1/8" wide. Have your local copy shop reduce a few of your cartoons to printed size to see if your lettering is still legible when reduced.

There shouldn't be too much writing either. People prefer reading shorter, quicker-paced comics.

Many aspiring cartoonists don't use waterproof drawing ink to finish their drawings. Pencils, ballpoint pens, and most felt-tip pens don't reproduce well enough for syndication. Aspiring cartoonists should learn how to use pens and/or brushes with waterproof drawing ink.

Finally, many aspiring cartoonists develop comics that are too similar to already successful strips. Newspaper editors aren't going to duplicate a comic that they already print.

HAS KING FEATURES SYNDICATE MERGED WITH NORTH AMERICA SYNDICATE?
Yes, King Features is made up of several previously independent syndicates. It includes Cowles syndicate and North America Syndicate, which was formerly called News America Syndicate.

Since your work is reviewed by the editors of all these syndicates, you need send only one copy of your proposed comic feature for consideration by King Features, Cowles and North America Syndicates.

Making Snacks

Addresses . . . advice . . .

US SYNDICATES

King Features Syndicate
(now merged with North American Syndicate
and Cowles Syndicate)
235 East 45th Street, New York, NY 10017
Tel: (212) 455 4000

Universal Press Syndicate
4900 Main Street, Kansas City, MO 64112
Tel: (816) 932 6600

United Media (United Feature Syndicate)
200 Park Avenue, New York, NY 10166
Tel: (212) 692 3700

Los Angeles Times Syndicate
Times Mirror Square, Los Angeles, CA 90053
Tel: (213) 972 5000

Chronicle Features
870 Market Street (Suite 1011),
San Francisco, CA 94103
Tel: (415) 777 7212

The Washington Writer's Group
1150 15th Street NW,
Washington, DC 20071
Tel: (202) 334 6375

Creators Syndicate
5777 West Century Boulevard (Suite 700),
Los Angeles, CA 9045
Tel: (310) 337 7003, ext 1987

Tribune Media Services
435 North Michigan Avenue (Suite 1500),
Chicago, IL 60611
Tel: (312) 222 4444

Adventure Feature Syndicate
Bill Barry
329 Harvey Drive (Suite 400),
Glendale, CA 91206
Tel: (818) 551 0077

Cartoonists & Writers Syndicate
67 Riverside Drive, New York, NY 10024
Tel: (212) 326 9256

ADVICE

That's Hall, Folks
Robin Hall/Peter Hall
345 Cregagh Road, Belfast BT6 0LE,
Northern Ireland
Tel: 01232 402049

Cartoon Critique
*A special consulting service, books and special
reports*
Bill Barry
329 Harvey Drive (Suite 400),
Glendale, CA 91206
Tel: (818) 551 0077

GUIDES TO THE MARKETS

USA

The Syndicate Directory
Editor and Publisher Magazine
11 West 19th Street, New York, NY10011

Artist's and Graphic Designer's Market
Writer's Digest Books
1507 Dana Avenue, Cincinnati, OH 45207
Tel: (513) 531 2222

UK and Europe

Writers' & Artists' Yearbook
A & C Black
35 Bedford Row, London WC1R 4JH
Tel: 0171-242 0946

Index

That's Hall, Folks!